APR 2 8 2021

Let's Talk About Hard Things

Anna Sale

SIMON & SCHUSTER
New York   London   Toronto   Sydney   New Delhi

Simon & Schuster
1230 Avenue of the Americas
New York, NY 10020

Names and identifying characteristics of some individuals have been changed.

First Simon & Schuster hardcover edition May 2021

SIMON & SCHUSTER and colophon are
registered trademarks of Simon & Schuster, Inc.

For information about special discounts for bulk purchases,
please contact Simon & Schuster Special Sales at 1-866-506-1949
or business@simonandschuster.com.

The Simon & Schuster Speakers Bureau can bring authors to
your live event. For more information or to book an event,
contact the Simon & Schuster Speakers Bureau at 1-866-248-3049
or visit our website at www.simonspeakers.com.

Interior design by Kyle Kabel

Manufactured in the United States of America

1   3   5   7   9   10   8   6   4   2

Library of Congress Cataloging-in-Publication Data has been applied for.

ISBN 978-1-5011-9024-7
ISBN 978-1-5011-9025-4 (ebook)

For Arthur

The values required for social repair are the same values required for personal repair.

—*Sarah Schulman*

I remind myself all the time now that if I were to have been born mute, or had maintained an oath of silence my whole life long for safety, I would still have suffered, and I would still die. It is very good for establishing perspective.

—*Audre Lorde*

Openness creates openness.

—*Ann Simpson*

Contents

Introduction

When I was thirty years old, words failed me.

I couldn't stop my marriage from unraveling, despite going to couples counseling and church, despite buying new relationship books and rereading passages I'd underlined in old ones. We'd been together since I was in college and had learned how to be adults together. We were best friends who loved each other. And then we were two people who couldn't be in the same room together.

At first the breakdown happened by such small degrees we didn't notice. Or rather, we noticed, but we didn't know what we were noticing. Each argument felt specific and isolated, but one by one they built up a lingering resentment that tore at our friendship. We tried to talk about it. We analyzed each individual argument and did our best to smooth over hurt feelings. I spent months trying to say everything I could think of that would recommit me to our marriage, re-endear me to him, and keep my life in line with what I thought it ought to look like.

That didn't work. Because, all the while, the underlying conflict went unsaid. Quite simply, we didn't want the same thing anymore.

Ours was a boring divorce. There were no real scandals. We had no children, no pets. My ex-husband and I mutually agreed to end the marriage. But it was still devastating and confusing. I couldn't explain what had happened, either to myself or anyone else. It would take years for me to make any sense of it.

This was new for me. I grew up with a certain faith that I could find the right words to navigate whatever life threw at me. I had two older sisters in college by the time I was in fourth grade, and they were always offering the long view on my pressing questions as I grew up: about friendships, drugs, sex, music. I just had to ask the right questions, and I could harvest their wisdom. I also kept notebooks scrawled with quotes from poetry, music lyrics, speeches, and books—scraps of insight to stow away for future use. When I became a political reporter at twenty-four, it was partly out of that same underlying belief, that with enough phone calls and stacks of documents—and the pitch-perfect question—I could uncover the truth and set the world right.

Sure, I knew it was a rosy view, but for a long time all my studying and digging and researching kept me feeling on track. That is, until I needed to decide whether to stay in my marriage, and what the hell to do if it was actually over. The answer was not something I could google. (I tried.) The truth was that no one else could tell me what to do. I needed to figure out my own choices and face the trade-offs that came with them.

What ultimately helped me to find a sense of clarity, little by little, was talking to other people about the choices they'd made when they'd felt lost. I had conversations with family members, friends, coworkers, and older mentors. They told me about their mistakes and where they got help when they needed it. They made me see how normal it is to find yourself grappling with uncertainty and despair. Theirs were messy stories, without neatly packaged lessons or aphorisms ready to be copied down in a journal. And, crucially, they made me feel like I wouldn't be alone as I began to figure out my next steps.

The stories stuck with me. Once I stumbled away from my marriage and began to put my life back together, I decided I wanted to keep having those deep conversations. I decided to make that my job.

I pitched my idea for *Death, Sex & Money* to my bosses at WNYC, New York City's public radio station, as a show about the things that mattered most in life but that we talked about least: how death and loss, sex and relationships, and money and work shape all of our lives. I came up with the name for the show while I was out walking my dog, and I smiled at its boldness. Then I thought, *What could be better? We flinch from these topics in public conversations, but they make up the most animating details of our lives!* As I got the show started, I noticed that when I explained the idea to my interviewees, they leaned in. I told them that I would be asking about the hardest, loneliest things all of us go through, in the hopes that others might listen and feel less on their own. Our conversations became open, collaborative, and honest. It was like uncovering a buried passageway to unexpected emotional connection.

For seven years, the show has given me permission to explore who and how we love, how we survive and scrape by, and, of course, the urgency of it all, because we don't get to be here forever. Many of us have fight-or-flight responses when uncomfortable things come up, but we also have a deep need to share. We all want to be understood, and we all want to look like we are handling setbacks, pain, and alienation gracefully. But life is not so simple, and it doesn't help to pretend that it is. With every episode on the show, my goal has been to give all of us a little more permission to try, mess up, and try again.

Hard conversations in real life, however, are a lot trickier than they are on a podcast. For one, they don't take place in a radio studio, between strangers, with an editing crew at the ready. They occur in real time, with the people we love, when our emotions are tangled and raw. When tensions are high, a single conversation has the potential to solidify a relationship into a lifelong bond, or to send it spiraling toward doubt. In that sense, there's a reason we like to spill our guts to bartenders and podcast hosts. Because it's downright terrifying to discuss the things that are most important to us with the people who are most important to us. Even so, the most meaningful moments of our lives hinge on the hard conversations we have with our family, friends, coworkers, and partners.

Living fully and honestly depends on stepping toward these conversations despite the risk. Hard things happen to all of us: family discord, illness, romantic rejection, missed opportunities, sudden loss. We each have different sets of resources to deal with these challenges—and for that matter, hardship is not evenly distributed among us; pain is often compounded by more pain. None of us, however, can navigate our way completely around life's difficult moments, especially on our own. Talking more openly about what we're facing helps us understand what is specific about each of our circumstances, and how our experiences fit into broader patterns that we can learn from and take solace in.

In these pages, I address five sweeping categories that contain many of the hardest conversations we'll have in our lives—death, sex, money, family, and identity. These subjects are all inescapable, and each is also challenging in its own particular ways. Over the course of each chapter, I'll share the stories of people who've lived through—and learned how to talk about—the challenges and pitfalls each subject presents. Throughout, I'll also share the most pivotal conversations I've had in my own life, and what I've learned while struggling to find the right words. All of the conversations you'll encounter as you read are drawn from original interviews conducted for the book, though I also sprinkle in a few moments from the *Death, Sex & Money* archives when they resonate with the discussion.

I want this book to feel, chiefly, like a companion. My goal is to open up that buried passageway between us, to let us connect and understand our lives more clearly. Through the stories of others who've been there, you'll see how to navigate life's rocky territories. You'll see how people came to express what they needed to say, and how to begin translating that to your own hard conversations. These stories, taken together, remind you that you're not doing this on your own. The rest of us are going through all this right alongside you.

Death, sex, money, family, identity—the subjects at the heart of this book are not new. For as long as human society has existed, we've been grappling with them generation after generation, and vast bodies of literature, art, and religious scripture are devoted to each. But what is new—in recent decades, in the United States—is that each of us is taking more of the burden of life's hardest conflicts onto our own shoulders.

We used to have institutions, rituals, and conventions that led us through the uncomfortable patches of life, so we were less reliant on individual communication skills. If you've ever been asked to perform the wedding ceremony for a friend, you know that comes with a mix of thrill and panic. When you are liberated from old models that felt overly rigid, it's then up to you to write your own script. I'm one generation removed from a small family farm, and I belong to the first generation of women on either side to try to sustain full-time work after becoming a mother. It's an incredible expansion of possibility. Still, forging ahead on your own can be isolating and overwhelming. "This much freedom leaves you on your own," George Packer observed in *The Unwinding*, his 2013 chronicle of generational change and economic transition in America. "Without solid structures, Americans have to improvise their own destinies, plot their own stories of success and salvation."

Our structures that used to stand in for hard conversations have eroded. Churches and religious institutions used to handle the ceremonies of birth, marriage, and death. In the last decade in the U.S., though, there have been declines in both regular church attendance and identification with any particular religion, and Americans' trust in religious organizations also hit an all-time low in 2019, according to Gallup polling. That disillusionment tracks with declines in confidence over time in institutions including government, the media, and big business.

Part of the reason so many of us mistrust our institutions is because many of us feel abandoned by them. We are living and working in an economy where, as Yale political scientist Jacob Hacker put it, there's been a "great risk shift" from government and institutions to individuals and families. More of us work for ourselves—more than a fifth of working Americans are self-employed or independent contractors—a trend that's been increasing for decades. The number of students who have to take out loans to pay for higher education has more than doubled between 2003 and 2019, meaning that many are starting their careers in a hole that previous generations never had to fill. Even when you do get a job with benefits, most company retirement programs no longer incorporate company pensions—it's just you, your individual 401(k) account, and the fluctuations in the market.

If you feel overwhelmed, it makes sense. If you don't know where to go for help, that does too. When the government and community institutions aren't there to help us to make sense of hard things, we rely on informal networks, the people in our lives, to help us make sense of what is happening and trade concrete information to help each other. But these social networks, our most basic relationships, are also under stress. Americans increasingly report feeling lonely, up to 60 percent in a survey released in early 2020, and that was pre-pandemic. Since then, Covid-19 has only continued to fray our communal fabric. With many workplaces and schools closed, and public gatherings restricted, each of us had to figure out our own individualized strategies to keep earning money, educate our kids, and care for sick loved ones—now from a distance. Yet as our lives collapsed to their most local level, we still lost trust in our neighbors. In the first weeks of the pandemic in 2020, more than half of Americans told the Pew Research Center that they believe most people in this country look out for themselves rather than helping others. And that loss of faith compounds. As Pew noted, "The less interpersonal trust people have, the more frequently they experience bouts of anxiety, depression, and loneliness."

The scale of the work that's needed is overwhelming. With the decline of community, civic institutions, and rituals, it's increasingly on individuals to rebuild connections on our own. Doing so means reaching out, supporting one another, and talking about the most difficult challenges we're facing. We are all figuring out how to have relationships, nurture our families, and find security during a time of so much upheaval. We are also all navigating a tilted landscape where inequality and racism stunt opportunities that many of us have in life, through no fault of our own. Addressing these larger problems takes political will, not just individual action, but both start from the same spark. When we share and listen to each other about our deepest hardships and needs, we start to see one another more clearly, and the connections between us are reinforced. This is true both within the tight-knit cloth of our families and the broader weave of society. Vulnerability softens us to one another, and it encourages humility more than self-righteousness. More concretely, when you share stories about how you've navigated dilemmas around identity, or money, or family, you're sharing knowledge that we can all build from.

There is a lot in life that is difficult, and there is no getting around that. Good conversation will not take away the shock of death or heal the sting of heartbreak. But isolation and stigma will inevitably make that pain so much worse. The willingness to talk is a salve that any of us can offer.

But how do we start a conversation that we know will be difficult? Where do we start?

From my own experience, as an interviewer and also in my personal life, I've learned that the way you approach a hard conversation either reinforces a pathway for exchange or erodes trust in the relationship. You can set yourself up for a more productive, less volatile exchange by being clear about what you are trying to accomplish by treading into challenging terrain. This is both the most obvious advice in the world and completely impossible to consistently follow. (Including for me. Just ask my husband.)

When you start a hard conversation, you will want to be able to say why you'd like to talk. First, you need to ask yourself why you want to have a conversation about something hard. Then, when you initiate, start by asking if it is a good time to talk, and explain why you want to have this particular conversation. *I've been wondering about something*, or *I need to tell you something I haven't*. With this groundwork, you are signaling that you want to go into a different mode together. Again and again, I have noticed during interviews that when I explain why I am asking a particularly sensitive question, people are much more open to answering it. They feel invited in, rather than ambushed.

As you talk, you need to pay attention to how you are relating to your conversation partner, even as you press on uncomfortable things. Notice their body language, or when their answers become short or clipped, and what makes them expand further. You are watching for cues about where you can push more, and what needs to be left for another time. This is the part of the conversation that is not about what you are hearing, but how you are hearing it. By paying close attention, you are tending to your relationship, the emotional dynamic between you, as you exchange words and ideas.

In other words, the chief skill in any hard conversation is how you listen. This might seem straightforward, something that any of us can do all day. But in all of my interviews, I've noticed how a conversation can either shrivel or bloom depending on how one listens. Often, in the course of a normal back-and-forth, we rush to fill any gap in the conversation. We step in to relate our own story, to show that we understand; or we start flinging out advice, to show how we can be helpful. "Most failures of listening are not due to self-absorption or bad faith, but to our own need to say something," family therapist and psychologist Michael Nichols wrote in his book *The Lost Art of Listening*. When we wait instead, when we give more space, we open the door for something new and intimate to unfold. The person you're talking to will notice when you really hang on to what they say, or repeat their words back to them for clarity. To feel someone listening to us is to feel deeply respected.

Sometimes, of course, the most difficult part of a hard conversation is knowing when to speak up and make yourself heard. It's nerve-wracking to claim the space to say something you've been silent about for years. And you do not have to talk about trauma or loss until you feel ready. For that matter, not every person in your life is an appropriate partner for vulnerable conversations. But when you put off speaking up because it might upset someone else, you are putting their comfort ahead of what you need. Choosing to change that dynamic is empowering. "I had refused to let the reality he was insisting on be my reality," poet Claudia Rankine wrote in her book *Just Us: An American Conversation*, about a moment when she decided to challenge a white man who was sitting next to her on a plane, after he insisted he didn't see color. "I was pleased that I hadn't lubricated the moment, pleased I could say no to the silencing mechanisms of manners."

Once you're in the thick of any difficult conversation, moving between listening and speaking up, the most important thing is to pay attention to your pacing. Some of my hardest conversations have felt like wild race-car rides, where my emotion swelled up into anger or hurt, and I felt briefly like I was careening out of control. Those swells have a purpose—they show me what is at stake and where I'm feeling most challenged—but their usefulness burns out quickly. I've learned that it's worth pausing when I'm on the verge of being overwhelmed, either to end the argument where it is if I need some time to reset, or to take a breath and downshift to a different, slower gear. One way to pull back is by trying to collect more information with an open question, or I'll just reflect out loud on the intensity of my response and ask what's provoking such a forceful reaction. Slowing down helps you consider what it is you are hearing, notice how you are reacting, and determine whether you agree. When possible, I try to end my hard conversations back near neutral, when I'm talking slower, listening more clearly, and my conversation partner and I can reemphasize why we wanted to have this hard talk to begin with.

In that sense, this book is not a manifesto for radical honesty. Hard conversations happen inside relationships, and relationships require their own kind of tending. I believe in kindness and striving for compassion, not spouting off regardless of the pain words can cause. This book is about using conversations to fortify our connections. Sometimes, that requires bringing up hard topics you need to discuss. Perhaps more crucially, it means listening when they're brought up to you.

I do not offer go-to words or phrases to mend discomfort, uncertainty, or disagreement. Plenty of business and self-help books offer bulleted lists for how to navigate high-stakes conversations with confidence. This is not that. What you'll read here are ways that I and others have found our paths through challenging subjects with the goal of creating more openness and stronger relationships, rather than achieving a particular outcome. The point of these conversations is to see more clearly, not to reduce the complexity of our relationships to a formula.

Still, it is useful to have some guidance on where to start when you're ready to take up the challenge of a hard conversation. To that end, as you move through these five chapters and get to know the details of people's lives, each section is delineated by a short sentence that proved helpful in clarifying or transforming a relationship. These are phrases that are useful, simple, and repeatable: *What I want has changed*, or *All I'm asking for is understanding*, or *Tell me that story again*. If you need a push, consider these small sentences as prompts, offering permission to you and others in your life to begin exploring the unspoken.

Once we open the door, these conversations can be life-changing. As Andrew Solomon wrote in his book *Far from the Tree*, "the absence of words is the absence of intimacy." When we let tensions fester, or allow familiarity to pass for understanding, we tend to leave parts of ourselves out of our most important relationships. We miss out on the opportunity to continue to grow. We lose track of who we want to be, and we can't share our full selves with those we love.

Talking directly about hard things also helps us come to terms with the limits of our control. The most difficult conflicts in our lives cannot be resolved easily, or at all. One-on-one conversations about money or identity will not resolve the tensions inherent in the differences between us. Talking about death will not undo its inevitability or the loss that comes with it. Often, acknowledging the limits of words can be one of the most important things you can say. "Words are amazing and they matter. Words can make a gigantic difference between carrying your pain or increasing your suffering," Megan Devine, a writer and grief counselor, told me. "And," she added, "words only point to something that is way beyond words and can never be touched by language."

That tension hums at the heart of this book. Throughout, our goal is to understand both the possibility and limits of hard conversations—how we can use words to describe, to compare, and to support each other through the parts of life that words alone can't fix. I want to assure you that anyone can build the skills to have empathetic and productive conversations, even if you feel like tough conversations aren't your strength. That's what we're going to do together here.

Death

I was sixteen years old the first and last time I saw someone die. I was at my grandparents' fiftieth wedding anniversary party in their community's Ruritan Club building. On the walls hung group photos of men, sometimes with my grandpa in the center, sometimes with my uncle Bailey, his brother. They switched off leading the club of local farmers in their small North Carolina town outside Elizabeth City, where their daddy had farmed and his daddy before him.

My family had driven down from West Virginia for the weekend, to celebrate my grandparents with everyone in their community—the farmers and their wives, the members of their church, the volunteer firefighters. Uncle Bailey was scheduled for a heart procedure the next week.

Bailey was my grandpa's younger brother. He had served in Europe before he took over his father's farm with my grandpa. When Bailey got home from the war, my grandparents had already started dating. That's how Bailey met my grandma's younger sister, who became his bride. The brothers and their wives raised their families in two brick houses, with just a cow pasture between them.

We'd just finished taking family photos, the cousins who'd been raised far away from the farm—my sisters and me, the "city girls"—alongside the cousins who lived there. The picture I remember best is my mom and her brother, smiling while they stood behind their parents, who sat in white folding chairs, the place of honor marking their many decades together.

As I eyed the dessert table at the front of the room, I noticed Uncle Baily there. He grabbed at the corner of the table as he collapsed. There was a scream. Then someone yelled, "June, June!" My mom's name.

She crouched at Bailey's side immediately. My mother is a physical therapist, and also the family member who remains uncannily calm in moments of crisis. My aunt, a nurse, and my dad, a doctor, got on the floor beside her. They started CPR. One-two-three. Breath, breath. One-two-three. Breath, breath.

Everyone else watched silently. Bailey's wife, my aunt Ann, sat in a folding chair just feet away. Her children gathered around her. My grandpa watched too. One-two-three. Breath, breath. One-two-three. Breath, breath.

Someone had called the paramedics. No one talked much, save for a few whispers about whether the rain outside would delay the ambulance. The EMTs arrived quickly, though it seemed like forever, and we all watched as they rolled in a stretcher and pulled Bailey's horizontal body up onto it. He didn't move. I remember his brown socks showing between the bottom of his pants and his dress shoes.

A few days later, we gathered again. The same people who'd been at the anniversary party filed into the chapel at a local funeral home. I wore my anniversary-party dress to the funeral—I'd only packed one. In the reception hall afterward, the same kind of dessert table awaited us, with the same portioned-out sweets on individual paper plates. We celebrated Uncle Bailey's life and said goodbye.

I later heard that the day he died, before he'd showered and changed clothes for the party, Uncle Bailey had helped deliver a calf. His dirty work clothes were still in the washer.

The next time I visited my grandparents' house, I noticed that the family photo taken just before Bailey collapsed was displayed prominently in their living room. I remember looking at everyone's smiles, how we didn't know what was coming. My grandma, though, was not going to hide the remembrance of her fiftieth wedding anniversary because Bailey died at the party. Getting a nice frame for an anniversary-party photo was what you did with group photos from a family reunion. Bailey's death had its own set of prescribed rituals: covered dishes were delivered, the minister put together a service, everyone gathered at the funeral home chapel and then processed in a line of cars to our family's section of the town cemetery.

It happened, it was sad, and it was natural.

I did not grow up in my grandparents' farming community, so this kind of proximity to death, and the ready-made rituals for marking it, were not part of my upbringing. While my North Carolina cousins lovingly raised pigs and sheep for the livestock fair knowing full well they'd be eventually slaughtered, I was the kid who picked out *Old Yeller* at the video store because of the Disney logo on the cardboard sleeve, and then, when the family dog gets shot at the end of the movie, tearfully demanded of my parents, "How could you let us watch this?!?"

Today, when I learn that someone I know is gone or grieving, it's not from local obituaries or phone calls but from texts and social media. Instead of gathering together in a church or funeral home, I most often experience death online. I'll click around for the context and details, then I'll end up leaving a clichéd message of care—one that cautiously tries to navigate the grieving people's religious views and my own. Sometimes I offer prayers, but more often I land on a secular message: I'm "sending my love" or "holding you in my heart." Then, the next time I talk to someone who also knew the person who died, we trade information about what we know to fill in any gaps.

And each time this happens, it feels like I'm improvising, like I don't know exactly what to do or say when. This makes sense, because I was not trained to deal with death this way. In my family, after a death, you would go to a service, and then you found ways to be helpful. As a kid, I remember pulling into an unfamiliar driveway and staying in the minivan while my mom delivered a casserole dish to the front door. This was at a house I'd never seen before, and would never see again. Someone had died, my mother explained, so we were bringing them dinner. This wordless care was how my mom reached out to people who were grieving or to those who themselves were at the end of life.

"The most important thing we can do to someone who is dying?" writer Anne Lamott advised. "Show up; listen; nod." But in my adult life, I live far from many people I love, and showing up at their doorstep is not always an option. My husband and I have two little kids and both work full-time, so we are doing well if we manage to cook for ourselves a few times a week. Suffice it to say, I have never delivered a casserole.

Our experience is more the rule than the exception these days. Across the country, people are gathering around death less frequently than in the past, and when we do come together to memorialize someone, it is increasingly done in individualized, do-it-yourself ceremonies. The funeral home industry in America, for example, is grappling with decreasing demand for both funeral services and burials. "We have become more transient and less traditional, so the notion of cemetery plots for families to visit holds less significance," US Funerals Online reported in 2018. The group reported that cremation was the choice in a majority of deaths, with cremation providers reporting that 80 percent of their business is "direct cremation." People are collecting the remains of their loved ones and taking it from there.

At the same time, we are less connected to houses of worship that have traditionally seen us through the hardship that any death brings. As of 2019, more than a quarter of Americans claim no religion, a segment of the population that has tripled in the last twenty-five years, coinciding with decreasing trust in religious institutions. Meanwhile, Americans' belief in some kind of afterlife has remained remarkably consistent, hovering around 70 percent since World War II. It's not so much that we are understanding death in a more secular way. It's that more of us are grappling with the meaning of life outside of religious institutions.

More personalized, individualized death ceremonies mean that communities of grievers have no guidebooks, rituals, or straightforward to-do lists to center them in their moments of greatest vulnerability. "After my mother's death, I felt the lack of rituals to shape and support my loss," author Meghan O'Rourke wrote in her memoir about her mother's death, *The Long Goodbye*. "I found myself envying my Jewish friends the practice of saying Kaddish, with its ceremonious designation of time each day devoted to remembering the lost person."

And then came Covid-19. We lost the ability to sit with one another at the end, or to gather and memorialize the people we were losing. People who belonged to houses of worship were no longer able to gather there. We weren't even able to follow Anne Lamott's advice, to just show up to accompany our dying loved ones. All we had were words and the seeming impossibility of knowing when and how to start that difficult conversation about death.

The pandemic accelerated trends that were already happening. We are now more on our own in navigating grief and healing in our relationships. When someone in my life died during Covid, and when people in my life lost loved ones during Covid, no matter how much I would have preferred to show up at a memorial service and offer a quiet hug, that wasn't an option. I had to step up and struggle for the words to acknowledge death and loss. I had to learn to talk about death.

The objective of hard conversations about death is to express care. Before death, with people who are aging or who become ill, we have to ask what kind of care they need and want. When death is circling, we express care for those who are leaving and those who will be left by telling them what they mean to us. When death has happened, we show care by grieving, checking in, and remembering together. That's what we can do.

Still, these exchanges are delicate. They are happening within newly fragile relationships, and you have to pay attention to pick when to listen and when to speak. What you need to say may be too painful for someone to hear. A dying person may not want to talk to you about how they are dying; that may be the last thing they want to consider, even as time runs out. A well-meaning friend might try to offer you comfort while you grieve, but be too afraid to acknowledge the finality of death. "You'll get through this," they say, unknowingly diminishing the loss instead of being able to sit with you in it.

We are often tentative in our conversations around death, so they end shy of real connection. Or we long to problem-solve our way around pain and loss or decline, but we can't. We have to just talk about, and witness together, what happens when death comes into our lives. It happens to all of us eventually. As William Faulkner wrote in *As I Lay Dying*, "It takes two people to make you, and one people to die. That's how the world is going to end." Death comes for each of us, and no words can change that fact. Skipping the conversation about death because the words aren't coming easily is shirking away from death's ultimate challenge: to use our time well and with intention.

But while death is unavoidable, it comes in many forms that change its meaning and impact. Death can be sudden or protracted, too early or at long last. It strikes through accidents, suicides, overdoses, or, most often, in hospital beds. We lose our partners, children, parents, and siblings; we lose pregnancies, coworkers, high school acquaintances, and famous strangers. How and when we encounter death reveals who is taken care of by our society and who isn't. I explore these distinctions in this chapter, but I try to avoid the silent hierarchical competition that can bog down discussions about grief and death. I treat all deaths equally, because if a person is grieving, a person is grieving.

Over the years, I've sought to learn from those who have navigated death and loss, trying to understand which kinds of words helped and which didn't. I've also talked to people in my own life about their losses and their fears of death, as a kind of challenge to myself to have conversations that I otherwise would have put off. They were helpful and elucidating, and also, unsatisfactory. I wanted to be able to feel better about loss, or impending loss, by acknowledging it. But this didn't work. Instead, I learned that

25

skillful communication about death starts with the awareness that nothing you say is going to fix it or make it go away. The best way to talk about death is to make room for that unsolvable sadness to just be there, to offer comfort and dignity alongside it, and to say what you need to say while there's still time.

"It's okay you're not okay."

After a death, we are left to find the right way to acknowledge it—and the gaping hole it leaves—with those we love. At a time of so much pain, we often cause more by withdrawing or trying to resolve death with a neat turn of a phrase.

"The glaring wrongness was just so stunning," Megan Devine told me of her casual conversations after her partner Matt drowned in a river at the age of thirty-nine. "Largely, the people that I expected to have better skills actually had really shitty skills."

Megan is a therapist and grief counselor who runs a wonderful website called Refuge in Grief. Its welcome page offers two buttons—"I am grieving" and "Someone I know is grieving"—to demarcate those two distinct experiences. For both audiences, her site's welcoming message concludes, "Some things cannot be fixed. They can only be carried." She urges people who are grieving or who are trying to care for those in grief to push beyond the urge to offer soothing platitudes, and to instead witness the horror of loss. "People feel really helpless in the face of someone else's pain and they want to make that pain go away so they can stop feeling so helpless," she told me when we talked. "If we could just stop pretending that things are fine, things would be a lot better."

Megan was a therapist before her partner Matt died, but it was that experience of loss, and the repetition of ham-handed condolences afterward, that made her reimagine her work "by shifting the focus from grief as a problem to be solved to an experience to be tended," as she wrote in her 2017 book *It's OK That You're Not OK*.

Megan's loss was sudden, unbelievable, shattering. She and Matt were hiking together in the woods outside Portland, Maine, in July 2009. After six weeks of rain, the river was higher than normal. Matt went in for a swim while Megan watched their dog Boris move in and out of the water. She was turned away from Matt briefly to watch the dog when she heard coughing and a call for help. She turned to see Matt clinging to a tree in the river, then letting go. Megan and the dog jumped in after Matt and they were swept about two miles downriver before they were able to climb out and call for help. Three hours later, rescue crews found Matt's body.

Megan did not know what to do next and neither did anyone around her. A social worker arrived along with the first responders. As soon as Matt's body was located, Megan told me, "The young crisis worker walked over to me and handed me this packet and said, 'Now that you're a widow, you'll need these resources.' That was the absolute wrong thing to say in that moment!"

Then came the series of wildly ill-timed assurances from many corners that she would "find someone else." That started as soon as Matt died, including at his funeral. The intention, Megan knew, was to comfort her that she would not be alone forever. But to her it sounded like a callous denial of the relationship she'd lost. "How that landed for me was, he was not replaceable. You can't fix the pain that I'm in right now by plugging another human into it," she explained.

Often the misguided comments came from her therapist colleagues, "because they thought they knew what they were doing because they were therapists." She remembered what felt like "unintentional condescension," including, initially, assurances that it was okay to be sad. "Like, one, I'm not stupid," she told me. "If you know me at all, I know it's cool to be sad after having just watched my partner die."

More than anything, she resented having her experience narrated to her by others, rather than just having someone stop, acknowledge, and listen. "People make an assumption about what you're actually struggling with, and then they solve that struggle for you, never having checked out if that's even real or relevant," she said. "I think that's a really common thing that happens for grieving people."

Megan knew that people were grasping for the right thing to say that might unlock some healing, or at least a smile. Still, people's clumsy attempts cut particularly deep because of the rawness of her grief. "When you're grieving, when your life just exploded, you've got nothing. You have no barriers, no stabilizers, no ability to roll with shit. You are stripped down. And everything is painful. So you notice stuff a lot more," Megan explained. "You are suddenly in a whole new world, but everybody around you thinks it's the same world. And everything they say that doesn't help really illustrates that gap even more."

For Megan, the conversations that felt the best were direct and honest. She remembers one short exchange with the owner of a local bookstore. They ran into each other at a café, the place where Megan had met Matt, so she was already electric with emotion when she stepped inside. As she waited in line for coffee, the bookstore owner came to stand beside her. "He said something along the lines of, 'He was a really great guy. I didn't know him very well, but I was very impressed with who he was,'" Megan remembered. "Then he said, 'I just want to tell you this is going to take a lot longer than anybody will tell you before you start to feel normal in any way again.'"

Then he got his coffee and left. "It was great to hear somebody tell me what I already knew to be true. It was a validation of reality," Megan said. "And to me, that is the best thing that you can do."

This instance was both nice and rare. Megan noticed how often people offered a cursory, "Let me know if you need anything," as they exited conversations with her. It may have been sincere, but it felt like they were foisting more responsibility on her. "A grieving person very often doesn't know what they need," Megan said. "You're trying to make something that can't possibly be real, be real. That's taking ninety-nine of your one hundred units every day. You can't figure out what you need, and then figure out which one of your friends might meet that need, and then work through the whole thing that you shouldn't ask for help because we're bugging people, and then call a person you deem safe in order to ask them and risk them saying, 'I'm sorry, I can't do that right now.' That is not going to happen."

But Megan also learned that even as she was in the midst of her own crushing grief, people needed to hear from her. Some, frankly, worried for her safety. One friend would text her every few days, especially when she hadn't heard from Megan, and Megan remembers that fondly for the way it bluntly navigated the awkwardness of the moment. "The text would say, 'I'm really torn right now. I want to respect your solitude and I understand that you know how to care for yourself and you will reach out when you're ready. I'm also worried about you because I know that this is crazy and I haven't seen any evidence that you're still alive.'" So her friend proposed a system: Megan could just text back an asterisk to show her friend that she was there and receiving texts, but just choosing solitude. And Megan would do that, responding simply with, "*."

In these text exchanges, they were circling around really scary, dark questions and fears with the simplest of exchanges. That is often how conversations that acknowledge death are. "They are not easy, but they are simple," Megan said.

Death is overwhelming but it is not very complicated. Someone was here. Now they are gone. And we will all eventually be gone too.

What is simple are the words to acknowledge this: *I'm so sorry. This is so sad. I miss him too. I wish this hadn't happened.* All of the other assurances that were meant to comfort didn't help. For Megan, it was the most honest, unflinching expressions of loss that made her feel the least alone.

"It's not just yes or no."

Megan experienced firsthand how bad we can be at talking about death when it strikes suddenly. Yet we can also fall short when we see death coming. There are times when the diagnosis of a life-threatening illness jump-starts the very conversations we need to have, but often we miss that opportunity. Instead, we're barraged by an array of medical options that could still *save* a life, which gets in the way of acknowledging death.

That's what Katie Couric described to me, on *Death, Sex & Money*, when she told me about the death of her first husband from cancer. As he was dying, she wanted to keep his spirits up and encourage his fight. "Looking back on it, there was probably a lot of dishonesty," she said. "I wish that I had had the courage to really talk to my husband about the fact that he was probably going to die."

When doctors are treating an illness, their conversations with patients and their families often circle around which interventions could be tried next. "Our reluctance to honestly examine the experience of aging and dying has increased the harm we inflict on people and denied them the basic comforts they most need," physician Atul Gawande wrote in his 2014 bestseller *Being Mortal*.

"We're not taught to talk to people about death. We're taught to talk about disease and possible cures or therapies for it," Fernando Maldonado, a primary care physician in Vallejo, California, explained to me. "This is even when patients are very, very ill." Fernando felt this absence of training acutely because, as he was becoming a doctor, his mother Angelita was going through breast cancer treatment. She'd been diagnosed when Fernando was a senior in high school, and while Fernando went through college, medical school, and the rigors of residency, his mother was in treatment, then remission, then recurrence, then more treatment. "For twelve years, she got better. She always got better," Fernando said. That made her death in 2016 feel sudden, even after such a long illness. "I think a lot of us were more prepared for my mother's death when she was originally diagnosed."

That's the curse that accompanies a long illness. You have time to prepare, and to start hard conversations about medical wishes and end-of-life care, but those conversations also have to be ongoing, as Fernando's family experienced. There are opportunities for the illness to retreat, for health to snap back, for those involved to experience glimpses of hope. That's why, with the diagnosis of a serious illness, acknowledging the possibility of death early can be so important, even when death is not at all imminent. You've said the hardest thing together, which creates more openness to evaluate all the complicated and ambiguous decisions to come.

In some ways, the Covid-19 pandemic shattered the illusion that doctors are always at the ready to try to stave off the end. As the global health community scrambled to understand the virus, lifesaving equipment was rationed, visitors were prohibited, and final goodbyes were said over FaceTime. There was no escaping the fact of our physical vulnerability and mortality, and those of our loved ones. We will never know just how many people with coronavirus died in the United States, as some people with chronic illnesses and respiratory distress simply opted to stay home, untested, to give themselves more control over where they died and who was with them in their final moments.

The choice is there for an ill person to refuse further treatment even when doctors offer other things to try, but you have to talk about that choice with your loved ones. Fernando's wife, Cynthia Maldonado, is an emergency room physician in the same hospital system as Fernando. She told me when she's working in the ER and a patient is unable to communicate, she has to rely on the patient's loved ones to direct the care. "The first words that come out are, 'Do everything,' because they feel like that's what you should do for a loved one," Cynthia said. She understands that to love is to want to protect and do all you can, though after years of practice and seeing where continuous interventions end up, she's learned to pause and remind them that doing everything medically possible has its own costs and does not mean their loved one will be the same person they were before they came to the emergency room. "I sometimes reiterate, 'I'm not asking you what you would like us to do. I want you to put yourself in the patient's shoes and think, *This is what they would want.*'"

Fernando was sitting next to Cynthia on the couch as she described these conversations with patients, and he wondered aloud how he must've looked to his mother's doctors near the end. "For ten years, she told us, 'I don't want any resuscitative measures.'" But when Angelita's health took a turn in the spring of 2016, her oncologist suggested trying one more round of chemotherapy to see if it might help. Fernando noticed his mother was weary. "I was torn," he said. "In a selfish way, you always want something else to be done even though you have this little voice saying it doesn't really seem right."

Together, Fernando's family and his mother decided to do one more round of chemo, though later he suspected his mother had agreed because she sensed it was what her kids wanted. The treatment made his mother so sick she had to go to the emergency room. "And the physician looks at us and he says, 'Why are you guys doing this to your mom? You guys are killing your mom!'" Fernando remembered. "Because in his mind, he sees a woman with a long medical history of cancer, who has heart failure and just got a chemo round. In his mind, he's like, *You guys are idiots!*"

Fernando also knew all the details in his mom's chart. "We knew exactly what was going on. We're just trying to kind of feel things out because it's not just yes or no." Looking back at pictures now, Fernando can see that his mother was close to death when they decided to do that last round of chemo. Her skin and her posture show that she was gravely ill, but he said, "In the moment, I just saw her eyes, and my mom's eyes were the same eyes that they had always been." He wanted to take care of her, and he also wasn't sure when it was the right time to say goodbye.

Being up close to someone as they die, even managing their care on a daily basis, does not necessarily mean that you are confronting the reality of their decline. In a 2009 journal article about grief and caregivers, Kathrin Boerner and Richard Schulz made the distinction between knowing versus feeling a person is going to die. Some caregivers, they wrote, "could feel prepared about the informational and pragmatic components, but yet feel entirely unprepared emotionally." That type of preparation requires separate conversations, between the dying person and their caregivers. Then, after the end, talking about the caregiving experience specifically—what was stressful about it and what was rewarding—can be an important part of grieving for the caregiver, Boerner and Schulz wrote.

That's been the case for Fernando. Since his mom's death, Fernando talks with his patients regularly about his mother. He wants them to know that some of their choices will not be clear-cut, and he admits to them that he thinks he and his family made some mistakes. When he starts this conversation, he told me, he begins gingerly, by asking what the patients know about their health, and he listens for openings. "If any of the patients say the word 'death' at all, then I switch over more toward, 'Well, let's start thinking about your ideas and what you imagine your end to be like.'" He wants them to get acquainted with the idea that they may need to make decisions when there's incomplete data and uncertainty about timelines. They may need to make hard decisions about ending treatment before they feel ready to say goodbye.

Fernando says these conversations don't always unfold the way he'd like. "Some patients don't take it too well," he admitted. But for him, talking about death with his patients has become a new kind of ritual, one that has helped him grieve for his mother and forgive some of the regrets he's had in hindsight about her care. Making medical decisions at the end, he knows, is a difficult yet unavoidable balancing act of expressing love, advocating for the best care, and letting go.

"Acknowledge it. Don't pretend it didn't happen."

Gathering together, and sharing pain in community, is an important salve during grief. But some deaths can be much more private, with murkier ways to find support and mourn. "I felt like no one knew what I was going through," my friend Lesley McCallister told me about losing her first pregnancy when she was at twenty-three weeks. Her child died before Lesley and her husband had a name. They hadn't known his gender yet and no one had felt him but her. "I didn't know anybody who had been that far along and had a stillbirth, who had to go through labor and have nothing to show for it at the end."

I remember when Lesley called to tell me what had happened. My body sank into a chair, and then I was still as she recounted the horrors of that day. At an appointment that morning, after a completely healthy pregnancy, the doctor couldn't find a heartbeat. Then more doctors came in to confirm. The fetus, for unclear reasons, had died. Her pregnancy was so far along that they recommended vaginal delivery. As they began inducing delivery, she remembers all the paperwork. "I was inundated. Here's a pamphlet about grief. Here's a pamphlet about afterbirth." And the hospital staff asked about a name. "I was just like, what am I going to name my kid who's dead?"

She was calling me after delivering her son. She was still in the maternity ward, in a room at the end of the hall, one with a waiting room separate from the rest of the maternity floor. Her parents and her husband's parents had been there to visit during the day. "Did you physically feel labor?" I naively asked later. "Oh yes," she said, then again, "yes." They decided to name him William, though she's always called him Will.

For a few hours after delivery, Will stayed in the room near her bed, under a warmer so he wouldn't be cold to the touch. A nurse came in during shift change. "And she just had this attitude like, *So, are you going to hold your baby some more?*" Lesley recollected. "And I just remember having this sense of, like, *I don't know how much I'm supposed to hold my dead baby. Am I supposed to hold him some more? I don't know what the answer is.*"

She was in shock, both physically and emotionally. She didn't know how to spend this short time with him. She did know, that evening in the hospital, that she needed to talk about what had just happened. "I purposefully called the people that I wanted to hear it from me, because I wanted a support network," she said. "So that if I called them in hysterics later they'd know why."

I was frozen by the crushing sadness of what she'd told me in that call. I couldn't believe this had happened. I couldn't believe this was asked of women. I couldn't believe this had happened to my friend. I had nothing to say, except to repeat, "I'm so, so sorry." I also remember sitting there hearing her shocked voice and wondering if Lesley would remember this moment as a time when I had been a good friend. Had I said the right things?

Of course, she wasn't really registering what I was saying. There may be wrong things to say, as Megan Devine said, but there is no *right* thing. The words don't matter much. It's most important that you're just there. When I asked Lesley about that night years later, no one's words to her stood out from those early phone calls. She remembered what time it was, around tip-off of an NBA Finals game, and feeling like she just wanted to tell people quickly so she could watch basketball with her husband in the hospital room. She remembered the waves of crying, then not crying, then crying.

Lesley is self-deprecating and more open than most. Her to-the-pointness has an air of efficiency to it. On that night, her directness was the only tool she had. Everything around her and everything she'd known was falling away. Telling the story, phone call by phone call, was the only measure of control she had. She was reaching out to say: *This happened to me.*

Acknowledging any kind of death is important. For parents who lose pregnancies, the death can feel even more urgent because the loss is invisible to the outside world. My friend Lesley initially tried to resume her normal routine after her stillbirth and took just a week off of work from a demanding job at a lobbying firm. About a month afterward, Lesley's mom gave her a gift certificate for a massage. And as Lesley lay on the table having her body pressed and pulled, she told her story again, and her massage therapist shared her own experience with stillbirth. Decades before, she'd delivered twins, and only one had survived. Lesley told me, "She said, 'I'm going to offer you one piece of advice: I buried my feelings and I didn't deal with my grief in a positive way. I just pushed it all aside. I had this newborn I had to be happy about.'" She warned Lesley that if she didn't cry when she was sad or get enraged when she felt angry, it would keep coming back, over and over.

This became Lesley's new assignment: to grieve. In front of people she knew, or people she didn't. It helped her, she realized, and also it might turn out that others in her life could relate and be helped by her sharing. Practically, this meant that Lesley was going to allow herself to fall apart in public. Whenever she felt emotion well up in her, she let her tears come. Trips to Target were a particular challenge. "I remember feeling like pregnant people were following me everywhere I went," she said, laughing in retrospect. "It did not matter which section of Target I was in. I would run into a pregnant person. I cried a lot at Target."

And Lesley also came to appreciate the advice, unwelcome as it felt at the time, to name their stillborn baby. They received a "Certificate of Fetal Death" that lists his given name—William Andrew McCallister. She likes having words to confirm that he was her first child and she is Will's mother. Over the years, she's appreciated the brave courtesy of others using his name too. "I really appreciate when they're willing to say his name out loud, because a lot of people don't want to upset you, but they don't realize you're upset anyway," she said. "You would rather that they at least acknowledge it than pretend it never happened."

Lesley and her husband have since had two more children, who have been raised knowing about their "big brother, Will, in heaven." They mention him in their prayers before bed every night, and every April they mark Will's birthday with an ice-cream cake. One year, when the cake decorator handed over the cake, she asked Lesley's son Luke if it was his birthday, and he proudly told her, "Oh no, it's my big brother in heaven's birthday!" The woman paused and gave a nervous smile to Lesley. "But it did kind of warm my heart. He was so proud," she said, her voice cracking. "I never wanted it to be a day when they thought, *Oh, this is when Mommy is depressed.* I didn't want them to dread it. Because as sad as it is and was, good has come out of it."

A lot of that good has come from Lesley's decision to be open about her grief. Her kids understand that death and sadness are normal. Other families who lose pregnancies have known that she's someone they can talk to about it. She estimates she's been alongside at least five moms as they have experienced the first waves of grief. Some of them were acquaintances through her church, some were strangers. When she hears these stories, often first through messages online, "My immediate feeling is, *I'm so sorry*, because I know the depth of that pain and the emptiness that exists." She says it feels heavy, like she needs to suit up in armor to retell her story. "Then I'm like, here's my opportunity to be there for somebody, because I didn't know anybody."

Still, she jokingly worries that she's been the morbid, weird mom who stops small talk cold when asked how many children she has. Three is true; only two are alive. When people ask, she's learned to say, "I have two children at home." Lesley told me her youngest child, Lydia, recently stopped while standing at the top of the stairs, and looked at Lesley. "Hey, Mommy, do you wish you had three children at home?" she asked. "And I said, 'Yeah, buddy, I do.' But I'm in a place where I've learned to appreciate those questions."

"How did they die?"

Death often leaves us with the question of *why*. Lesley learned that her son Will likely died in utero from a cord accident no one could have predicted or prevented. There will never be a satisfying why.

When we hear about someone's death, or are grieving ourselves, the instinct to chase down the details of what happened is natural. It can also be a way of distancing ourselves from their fate and denying that death is also coming for us. Did they smoke? Were they older than me? Did they make a mistake, we tell ourselves, that we wouldn't?

Chasing down these details about the where, when, and why, Freud wrote in 1915, "We betray an effort to reduce death from a necessity to a chance event." We sense the unseemliness in ourselves. It's why this kind of curiosity is considered gauche. When I am that person who wants to ask, *What happened?* I've learned to do it in hushed tones, or at least not in the Facebook comment feed. Or with euphemism. Like, *Was it sudden?* Doing otherwise can feel like I'm dishonoring the dead or trying to dig up some gossip.

There are important reasons, though, to openly acknowledge the circumstances around death, that serve both personal and public functions. It helps us face stigma, like substance abuse or mental illness. It helps us see who is getting the care they need and who isn't. In the United States, life expectancy declined for the first time in fifty-five years in 2014, led by increased death rates for people in midlife from "deaths of despair"—drug overdoses, substance abuse, and suicide—along with "various organ system failures." The study investigated many reasons why. Income inequality, limited access to primary health care, and insufficient mental health care across racial groups contributed to this nationwide rise.

How we live in this country tracks with how we die. We saw this again with the data about Covid deaths in the United States. Black Americans died at twice the rate as white Americans. Native Americans and Latinos also had higher death rates compared to whites. And poor people died at higher rates. "The greatest predictor of coronavirus deaths appears to be income," *American Prospect* magazine summed up in July 2020, citing an analysis that showed death rates two and a half times higher in low-income New York City neighborhoods than in rich neighborhoods.

So the ability to prioritize politeness about causes of death comes, in some ways, from privilege. Some of us can look away, and some of us can't.

"I'm surrounded by death. People in my community die all the time, either by gunshot wounds or knives or by neglect," Alicia Garza, the Oakland-based cofounder of Black Lives Matter, told me in an interview. "Whenever I have to talk about the undignified ways in which people die, there is a grieving process for me personally. And alongside of grief comes a deep rage where you start to recognize, deep in your core, that the way that a person died was not a natural death, and it was unnecessary."

After George Zimmerman was acquitted of the murder of Trayvon Martin in July 2013, Alicia went online and posted "#blacklivesmatter." A few minutes later, another post: "Black people. I love you. I love us. Our lives matter." Her clear, blunt words helped launch a movement, and they were motivated in part by her exhaustion with the ways we fail to talk directly around death in our culture.

Death is something Alicia has been attuned to since she was a sixteen-year-old high school student, she told me, when she signed up to take a college course at UC Berkeley called "On Death and Dying." "I was a really angsty child. Super angsty," she said with a laugh. "I may have been a little bit obsessed with it."

By that time, her grandfather had died, "and I was his favorite," so she was acquainted with mourning and grief. Alicia wanted to explore the ways Western societies, and the United States in particular, try to keep the reality of death at a distance.

"Americans dance around death in the same way that we dance around race or other inequalities that exist in our society," Alicia said. Euphemisms for death like "passing on" or "off to a better place" obscure the conversation, she explained, in the same way that debates about race and inequality get sidelined by ignoring differences. While these kinds of expressions around death can be sincere expressions of religious belief, as well as ways to more gently describe death in tender moments, they can also downplay loss or, when someone dies an unnatural death, conceal what's been unjustly taken. "If we're using all the codes, then we don't get to who is responsible. We don't get to actually grieve properly, and we continue to pass on the trauma of the unresolved by being really dishonest about what's happening."

Alicia believes that the ability to confront profound injustice in the United States requires unflinching language. She offered Walter Scott, a Black man in South Carolina who was shot in the back by a white police officer in 2015 after a traffic stop, as a good example. "Walter Scott did not 'pass on to the other side.' He was murdered by a police officer, in an unjust and undignified way for no reason," Alicia said. "And we have to be able to say that in order to get to, 'Okay, what do we do about it?'"

On the internet, any of us could witness the death of fifty-year-old Walter Scott. After he was pulled over for a broken taillight, a passerby filmed him running away from police officer Michael Slager, who shot several times from behind before Scott stumbled to the ground. The video went on to show Slager cuffing Scott and walking to pick up and drop a Taser near Scott's limp body.

A federal judge later called the shooting "reckless, wanton and inappropriate" and sentenced Slager to twenty years in prison.

These kinds of video images have been an important driver in the conversation about racism, justice, and law enforcement in America, but the graphic and ubiquitous nature of death footage can be divorced from the emotional impact of death, and the humanity of the (mostly) Black men whose dead or dying bodies we've watched up close. Walter Scott, George Floyd, Eric Garner, Alton Sterling, and Philando Castile: the images of their deaths are so accessible, easily pulled up right in the palm of our hands. There's a tension between bearing witness and seeing it too up close. When we don't see people dying, their loss can be invisible. When we see it so graphically, Alicia told me she worries about another kind of death: "the death of dignity, and its impacts on Black people in particular," Alicia said. "I can't actually watch the images anymore. I know what those look like so I have to make choices about what I carry every day to keep going and do what I do."

Alicia told me she also worried about how a lack of public notice or the unavailability of footage of some kinds of deaths, like intimate partner violence, distorts our understanding of who is vulnerable. "I'm very conscious of how our mass understanding of death makes some bodies visible and other bodies invisible," Alicia said. "Part of the struggle is to not be desensitized to it." Not being desensitized requires feeling the full weight of the person's loss and mourning it, Alicia said. Every unjust death deserves commemoration alongside protest. "It's not just words. Like, I cry," Alicia told me. "I do a lot of ritual to celebrate them, to celebrate their life, how they helped me grow or learn something about myself, and then end up thinking a lot about, what am I carrying forward?"

Alicia told me that she learned to make space for grief after the death of a close friend, Joy de la Cruz, who died in a car accident just after they both finished college. Joy was a poet and was on a cross-country road trip to move to New York. Two days before the accident, she'd called Alicia when she was coming through Oakland. "And I blew her off. I just wasn't in the mood and I was tired," she remembered. Then she got the call from Joy's sister, telling her the news, and Alicia had to then tell all their mutual friends. "I was having a lot of different kinds of emotions—guilt, shame, anger, sadness. And then, every time I had to tell someone, it was just a constant reopening," she said.

Moving through all those feelings was overwhelming and confusing, but she didn't retreat, and she didn't do it alone. Instead, Alicia opened her home in Oakland to host a memorial gathering. Friends of Joy's came together for a funeral, and then they just kept hanging out. "We spent, like, a week together." For years afterward, the same group would gather in the Bay Area on the day of Joy's death, even if they hadn't been in close touch throughout the year. "And a lot of different things came out of that. People found each other, fell in love," Alicia said. "That open kind of vulnerability creates openings for a lot of things to come forward."

"I love you. How are you doing?"

There's another way death enters our lives, not by who it takes from us, but by the way it whispers its approach, with aging. We mourn getting older because it means there's less time left.

I've thought a lot about this since I became friends with Ann Simpson, whom I met when she was eighty-two. Our limited time together has always been a subtext of our friendship. I see her every few months, so incremental signs of decline are noticeable. It fills me with dread, the sort that I feel in my body before and after our visits together.

I first met Ann over the phone, when her husband, Al Simpson, the former U.S. senator from Wyoming, called me at the request of my now-husband, who was at that point my ex-boyfriend. What started as Arthur's wild Hail Mary to get us back together became the start of our marriage, the subject of one of the first episodes of *Death, Sex & Money*, and a very special friendship with Ann.

When I was thirty-six weeks pregnant with our first daughter, Arthur and I unexpectedly became neighbors with Al and Ann. We had decided to spend my maternity leave in Cody, Wyoming, where Arthur had long done wildlife fieldwork. After our daughter June was born, Ann and Al were the first visitors after my parents. (They brought a silver rattle and a pair of pink cowgirl boots.) Ann organized dinner drop-offs with women in town for our first week home from the hospital. Through that long summer of naps and walks with the baby carrier, I'd often catch Ann out in her yard. She'd invite me in for lemonade, and we'd sit in her kitchen, where she'd admire my newborn's ears and share stories about how she managed the demands of working while raising three kids.

During that summer, I noticed Ann's clothes getting a little looser. She'd make passing references to stomach troubles, a bug that wouldn't let up, and would demur on a helping of seconds. Not much more was said about it. But after our times together, I would feel a quiet panic that I hadn't adequately thanked her for making us a meal or for helping me so much in those first tender days of motherhood. I would try to explain the feeling of urgency to Arthur, but my anxiety didn't make sense when I said it out loud. Slowly, I realized that I was overwhelmed with gratitude for our friendship, and I was becoming terrified of not having enough time together.

Just before I went back to work, Arthur and I left Cody and moved to California. Months passed as we adjusted with fits and starts. We intended to visit Cody but never got to it. Thankfully, Al would be visiting Berkeley to give a series of talks, so we scheduled to see the two of them then. When they arrived, it didn't take long until we learned that in the months since we'd seen them, Ann had been quite ill. "I thought, *Well, I have colon cancer*," she told me. "Selfishly, I thought, *I hope I don't go through a lot of pain*. It was not a comfortable thing to think about, but being a practical person, I began thinking about who I would give my jewelry to, of all the stupid things."

Somehow, I had the idea that once you're in your eighties, you're more intimately acquainted with your own mortality. But over dinner during that Berkeley visit, Ann told me, when her illness made her so tired and weak, she realized for the first time, really, that she would die. During the listless evenings when she wasn't feeling well, she picked up a book that someone had given her, *Intimate Death* by Marie de Hennezel, a French psychologist who worked with end-of-life patients. "And I found it so comforting!" she said. "The fact that the end of life does not have to be a terrible experience."

I bought a copy of the book and could see what Ann meant. As de Hennezel described her interactions with friends and patients dying of AIDS and cancer, I was struck by the simple observations that captured the immensity of confronting death. "Even when one enters helplessness, one can still love and be loved," she wrote of one dying patient. De Hennezel talked of her conversations with the dying, of not having the words to respond to their urgent questions about what was happening—and what would happen next. "You don't know all the answers, but they have the right to ask all these questions."

She also described the clear objective that emerges as death's imminence is accepted. "Before dying," she wrote, "the person will try to leave his or her essence with those who remain—a gesture, a word, sometimes just a look to convey what really counts and what thus far has been left—either from inability or inarticulacy—unsaid." In this time of letting go, she witnessed not just a personal acceptance of the end, but the urge to communicate it to the people they were leaving behind. Even when our ability to talk is diminishing, we want to have one last conversation about what's most important.

But all of this comes after the acceptance that death is happening. Up until that point, there is often anger and denial. As de Hennezel wrote, "Mourning the loss of one's autonomy is one of the most agonizing tortures there is." This, I feel, is an important factor in how we should approach the subject of death with someone who is aging. Decline is embarrassing. Diminishment is visible. Your ability to do what you always did slides away. "Illness lays claim to many things and privacy is one of its first casualties," psychiatrist Harvey Max Chochinov wrote in his book *Dignity Therapy*. The same goes for aging.

Proximity to death becomes obvious, even when it's unspoken. That social awkwardness is what led Chochinov to devise the practice of "dignity therapy," a way of capturing the lessons, stories, and regrets a dying person wants to communicate. The dying person is in command. When they are losing control over so much else, the act of listening to them confers essential dignity.

The idea that asking about someone's experience confers dignity is what helped me summon the courage to ask Ann if I could interview her for this book, specifically to talk about her illness and her thoughts on death. I was back in Cody a few months after we'd last seen each other in Berkeley, and even though she'd declared herself on the mend from her bout with illness, I was increasingly worried that I needed to express more clearly how much she meant to me. I didn't want to miss my chance.

When I asked, she agreed without hesitation. And so we sat at her kitchen table, with two glasses of lemonade, to talk about her death.

She told me she had finally gotten a diagnosis of *C. diff*, a gastrointestinal infection, and after treatment was no longer losing weight. She was feeling better enough to start referring to her illness in the past tense. But she was down twenty pounds, which made her still look frail. I asked her to tell me more about what she'd learned while reading about a French hospice clinic during a long Wyoming winter.

"They all suddenly treated me as though I was dying!" Ann said. When she was at her sickest, she was open about it with her grown children, but tried not to make a big deal out of it. "I don't like to tell them too much," she said. "I don't like them treating me like an old person because I don't think of myself as an old person."

Ann comes from a long line of sturdy, self-sufficient people. "My grandmother broke her hip because she was so darned independent. She wouldn't let anyone help her into a chair," she said. "Now that I am the age I am, people try to help me. It's a reminder that I'm old, but because I don't feel old, it's sort of a shock."

When help is offered, she doesn't always appreciate it. "It reminds me not to do that with other people," she said. Over the years, she told me, she'd learned to offer an arm when she was walking next to someone who is frail, and to subtly pull it back if they waved it off. "But you can stand close to them in case they fall," she said. "It's a very delicate thing."

Ann shared how she'd honed a kind of respectful directness about death from giving care for others. She told me about a ninety-nine-year-old friend who was in the hospice at the local hospital. In her younger days, Ann told me, her friend had been an actress with looks that caused men to swivel their heads after her whenever she passed. When Ann went to visit her dying friend in her last days, "she had whiskers all above her upper lip." So, during her visit to the hospice, Ann asked her friend gently if she could bring her tweezers the next time she visited. "Oh, would you?" her friend replied. Ann spent the next visit plucking.

Being on the receiving side of the care, though, embarrassed Ann. "I felt that I had taken my life and my good health for granted, and been a little judgmental perhaps about other people's illnesses," she admitted to me. Ann's father died of brain cancer when she was fifteen, leaving her mother with teenage twin girls. Ann integrated the fact of life's tenuousness into her no-nonsense approach to life. "When [Al] would go on a trip, I would always spend my time thinking, *What would happen if he were killed?*" she told me. "My father did die and my mother wasn't prepared. I always prepared for the worst."

But, until she'd gotten ill, that didn't include preparing for her own death. She told me she still hadn't written out the list for her jewelry or the letters to her children telling them each what they mean to her. "I was so tired," she said. She played solitaire and talked with Al at their kitchen table. "He was very fearful.

But it was a very happy time for me when I wasn't feeling well because Al was kind and attentive."

Grand pronouncements and to-do lists didn't help; quiet company did. She also thought about why she wasn't ready to die. "What I think about when I think of dying is, *I really want to see my grandchildren grow up*. That's what I want," she said, her voice cracking. "I don't want to miss anything."

I asked her how she ended her visits to her older friend in hospice. "Each time I left I said, 'I love you. I'll see you on the other side someday.' And then I'd go by and she'd still be there!" Then Ann paused a beat while her eyes moistened. "And then I went by one day and the room was empty and the clothes were all packed."

That day, over lemonade with Ann, I ran out of questions before I felt like I had gotten all the answers.

I did tell her, haltingly and clumsily, how I sometimes felt anxious that we'd only met once she was in her eighties, and I noticed how that made me want to hold tight to every conversation we had. "This is so special," I told her, trying to stuff into a few words how much appreciation I had for her and our relationship.

With her characteristic lack of muss, she took it in with a nod. That was it.

"Is there anything else you need to know?"

A few days after I had sat down in Ann Simpson's kitchen and discussed death over lemonade, I ate lunch with her daughter Sue. Sue and her mom are close, but Sue does not like to talk about her mom's mortality. Over salad, I started awkwardly telling Sue about my interview with her mom, and just like Ann described, when I mentioned death, Sue put her fingers up to her ears and started humming. This is what she does when her parents' deaths come up in conversations, she said with a laugh.

I laughed too, and then, as I offered some rough outlines of why I'd wanted to talk to Ann, Sue's eyes got glassy and red. Here I was, a recent friend of her mom's, being the jerk who's describing *my* fear of her mother's death. Sue listened, and told me that, for her, she worries that lingering on her parents' deaths will mean wasting time. "I know it's going to happen, but why focus on that while we have this time?"

It is an important point. We are all going to die, but knowing that doesn't mean we all need to sit around like a bunch of goth teenagers reading Nietzsche. There is the danger of getting trapped in neuroses, in cycles of dread. The ideal, I believe, is finding a way to weave the acknowledgment of death alongside an ability to not dwell on it too much before its time. This is true of conversations about death, and also of the pain and suffering present in life generally. As my grandma showed with her framed photos, it is possible to face death in the moment and still fondly remember the party.

Over lunch, Sue gamely shifted the conversation away from her parents and started describing a memorial service they'd all just attended the weekend before down in Jackson. A friend she'd known since college, Shelley Simonton, had died of melanoma eighteen months after discovering a lump in her underarm. On a late-summer afternoon, hundreds of people gathered on a local cattle company's land. There was a tent, rows of chairs, and a line of porta-potties, the "nice" kind, as Shelley had requested.

Shelley had planned the whole service in the last weeks of her life, including assigning particular topics to a list of speakers.

Her cousin was to talk about Shelley's family, one friend was to talk about skiing and her love of the outdoors, and her younger brother, Mike, could talk about whatever he wanted. That was the eulogy Sue remembered. She told me some of Mike's jokes, like the way they'd adapted rock anthems for Shelley's final days. He assured his sister he was going to lead the crowd at the funeral in a rousing rendition of "Don't Stop Bereaving."

Mike was Shelley's only sibling, five years younger, and though they'd lived in different states since college, they were very close. About six weeks after the memorial service, I called Mike in Chicago, where he works as a manager for Fitch Ratings. He readily shared the twenty-minute slideshow he'd put together for the memorial. Backed by folky songs and power ballads, it showed Shelley as a child, Shelley smiling openmouthed in football stands as an adult, Shelley getting married, then Shelley getting an IV infusion of chemo, Shelley at a wig shop, and Shelley, gaunt in a hospital gown, leaning over to hold her dog's face in her hands.

Mike told me that when he put together this slideshow, he was following his sister's lead in being specific about what had happened to her. This was how she had dealt with her illness. Up until a few months before she died, she had chronicled her cancer treatment online on CaringBridge, a social media site designed to update loved ones during a crisis.

At the end of March 2016, in a post called "Journey Takes a Turn . . . ," Shelley recalled her appointments going back a few months, the chemo and the surgery options and the radiation, leading up to the conversation she'd had with her doctor about her latest scans. "The news is not good," she wrote. The mass under her arm was not shrinking. "My tumor is huge and sort of coming through the skin. It starts to bleed from broken blood vessel ends that are now exposed," she wrote. "The bleeding is dramatic and intense . . . The first time it happened it filled my shirtsleeve with blood and was uncontrollable." She described her husband, Matt, having to use Drano after blood plugged up the sink. And, she continued, the latest round of treatments was not working. "Melanoma is known for spreading, being aggressive, and beating the treatments. Mine has been especially aggressive." She concluded, "As such, I am no longer doing any cancer treatments."

This was the last post Shelley wrote on CaringBridge. Months went by. There was no post on the day of her death. Loved ones pitched in afterward to write about one last trip Shelley and Matt had taken to see whales off the Washington coast. The final posts, by her brother, Mike, invited everyone to Shelley's funeral.

When they all gathered, Mike stood before the crowd wearing sunglasses and a University of Wyoming baseball cap. He told them that the period after Shelley's terminal diagnosis "is kind of a missing piece for a lot of the people. I hope to demystify that a bit." He told them after months of "gutting it out, white knuckling it through whatever we faced, the terminal diagnosis was like a dam broke." For him, the emotions included "some selfish ones," he said, most notably "a profound sense of personal failure." He had told his sister they were going to get through this together, and now they knew she wasn't. "I was disgusted, embarrassed, and humiliated with myself."

He felt like he needed to apologize. They were sitting on a couch in Shelley's house, both of them facing straight ahead. Mike had his arm slung around her. "It wasn't supposed to be this way," he told her. "Maybe it was?" she answered. Mike got indignant, dug in, and they went back and forth as only siblings can.

Finally, Shelley told him, "You can believe whatever you want to believe," then she paused, relaxed. "There might be something bigger happening here that's beyond what you can comprehend."

Then she asked him to make her something good to eat, since she likely only had a few weeks left with solid food.

The next morning, they ran through her medical directives, and while Shelley called family and then friends about her new terminal status, Mike started a spreadsheet with all of her insurance policies, the beneficiaries, her passwords, and answers to security questions. They split up what needed to be done, Mike said, "her sitting over on the couch, me over at the kitchen table." Friends of hers started coming to visit, one after the other, as they heard the news. Mike would sometimes interrupt them, like to ask about a policy number or to get Shelley to follow up on the password reset on her phone. "We kind of had our game faces on, from the perspective of, we need to get this done." It was nice to have tasks, even death-focused ones, to distract them from what was looming.

Shelley then moved on to a new spreadsheet: the run of show for her funeral.

And so, two months later, in front of hundreds of people, Mike described one of her last nights alive. They were in the phase where hospice workers were visiting regularly. Matt had gone to bed after another long day of caregiving, so it was just Mike and his sister. She had to go to the bathroom and she warned him she might need assistance.

"A few minutes later she called out, 'Hey, buddy! I need help getting off the toilet,'" Mike wrote in his eulogy and shared with the assembled crowd. "We fastened the stomach bag to her shirt. We had her hold the morphine canister in her right hand. I squatted down on her left side and held her free left hand, the strong hand, close to my body. We leveraged her little rear end up enough off the toilet seat so I could slide my right arm under her to scoop her up all the way. I kept looking away until she said it was okay."

Then Mike told everyone how she pulled up her polka-dot stretch pants and shuffled to the sink to brush her teeth. He jokingly asked if it was necessary. "I want to have fresh breath when Matt kisses me in the morning," she replied. That was when it all hit Mike. "I stood behind her leaning against the wall by their shower and bawled my longest, deepest cry since I was a young child," he said. "Shelley looked at me in the mirror while she was brushing—she had a way of giving me a hug with just a look—that's the look she gave me. Then she looked away and gave me space."

Shelley was helping Mike face her death, and did not try to soften its blow. "She could've turned around and given me a hug but she just continued brushing her teeth," Mike told me later on the phone. It felt like Shelley was prompting him to begin "pre-grieving," setting him up to mourn with honesty. That's different, he said, from what people call *healing*. "I don't feel like closure is a goal for me, like moving on and going back to whoever I was before. I'm not trying to return to who that person was," he told me.

His time together with Shelley in her last days gave him that gift. As she went through the to-do lists and led them into candid conversations about her end, Shelley forced them both to see their time together was really ending. Since Shelley's death, Mike has talked to other people who've lost siblings, including a close friend. She told Mike something that stayed with him. "She said, 'I've learned to carry my grief around like my iPhone or anything else. It's just something that's with me and I don't fight it.'" It helped Mike to hear that, because being with Shelley in her final months and days did not dull the pain of her loss. She was still gone. What these moments with his dying sister provided was a reckoning with death. "Moving from the surreal to the reality of it all," he said. "I do have disbelief, but I'm able to kick myself out of it pretty fast because I witnessed that and was present for it."

That's what our predominant experiences with death miss. When we don't talk about death, what it means, and how it takes from us, our grief is incomplete. Death is incredibly personal, and at the same time it is a shared experience. That's what Mike wanted to bring to Shelley's memorial service. "I was just trying to picture how surreal it must be for them, outside of the close proximity, to not really witness the decline, to not really have anything be disrupted in their daily lives, and then try to also feel that there has been this sense of loss. It would be so hard." They did not have a visitation, so without her body as proof, Mike felt a responsibility to make Shelley's death real with words.

―――――――――――

Death is inconceivable, an end we can witness but cannot know. This is true when we are distanced from it, whether by hospital waiting rooms or in front of a screen, or even when it happens right in front of us, like Shelley's last hours with her family or my uncle Bailey's sudden collapse. The poet Elizabeth Alexander found her husband at the base of a treadmill, gave him mouth-to-mouth, lay on top of her husband's body at the hospital after he was declared dead. And still that question remained. "I lost my husband. Where is he? I often wonder," she wrote.

There is a skill to talking about death with care. It takes openness and a willingness to be awkward. But more fundamentally, these hard conversations are about finding some measure of acceptance that death exists. Even the most artful elegy won't protect us from missing the ones we love, or our loved ones from missing us. Yet there is an enormous difference between expressing that love while there's time and missing your opportunity.

When the writer Cory Taylor was dying of cancer, she volunteered to go on an Australian television show called *You Can't Ask That*. "The questions, as it turned out, were unsurprising," she later wrote in the *New Yorker*: "Did I have a bucket list, had I considered suicide, had I become religious, was I scared, was there anything good about dying, did I have any regrets, did I believe in an afterlife, had I changed my priorities in life, was I unhappy or depressed, was I likely to take more risks given that I was dying anyway, what would I miss the most, how would I like to be remembered?"

When you're struggling for words, that list is a great place to start. When you ask someone who is dying any of these questions, you invite a moment of acknowledgment that death is coming. You're honoring the dignity of their life and soliciting their wisdom. The trick here is timing, and listening to the cues of the person you're talking to. This is what Fernando Maldonado has learned to do with his patients. While he listens for guidance on how deep into the conversation they are ready to go, he asks the first question because they might never initiate the talk on their own.

And if big questions get tiresome or you can sense that an ailing or frail person in your life doesn't want to face those big questions yet, you can lend comfort in small, useful ways to make things easier. Offer an arm when you're walking alongside someone, as Ann Simpson did, and tell them that you love them when you part. When the end is close, you can ask about something as concrete as computer names and passwords, like Mike Simonton did. Because while it may seem morose to acknowledge that death is coming, it is also caring.

When we crack the silence around death, it allows the love to rush in. Talking helps us capture the story of a life and how that person feels about it, just as the narrative arc is coming to an end. As the former *New York Times* obituary writer Margalit Fox described, "People have a primal fear of death, but ninety-eight percent of the obit has nothing to do with death, but with life." Facing death, for both the dying and those whom they're leaving, lets you declare both the impact you've had on each other's lives and how much you will miss each other. It clears space for conversations that will be your last memories together, and those are the sort of memories that hang on.

You don't always have that opportunity, though, when death comes suddenly or when the dying person is no longer lucid. You may not get to say what you want to say or wrap up all the complicated threads of a relationship. These kinds of death can leave our emotions more tangled, with grief and sadness mixed with anger and denial. Sometimes, we are left questioning why in ways that, as Alicia Garza said, lead toward more painful truths. Words alone will not staunch that pain. We may have the impulse to say something to fix, heal, or keep things positive. Death shows us, though, that words can't do any of that.

What words *can* do is describe what has been lost, as Megan Devine said. So instead of trying to smooth over discomfort, offer sympathies or a memory. Try not to disappear. Check in. And, if the opportunity presents itself, give a thoughtful gift. After her son's death, Lesley McCallister told me that some family friends of her parents, who had lost their own child to a stillbirth decades before, sent over a lilac bush that blooms in early April, around the anniversary of her son Will's death.

But even with all the best intentions, hard conversations about death require admitting that you are going to make mistakes. By its nature, a death in your life changes the makeup of your reality. It changes your relationships—who you go to for support, who is safe, who is stable. Everyone who is grappling with a death is absorbing it, from those closest to the death to those with more tangential relationships. Everyone is fumbling around and facing the grim reality there's no getting around this hurt.

Shelley Simonton recognized this in her last months and weeks, that there was only so much that words could do. "There's no official payoff or benefit to worry," she wrote in January 2017, a year after she first found a lump and less than five months before she died. "You don't get ahead of the pain because you worried for an extra few days."

It's the same when talking about death. You don't get ahead of the pain, but by talking with someone else you can find companions in that pain, to help beat back the particular isolation of death. That's what Shelley did in her conversations with her brother, her husband, her parents, and her friends in her final weeks. "Do I need to tell you anything else?" she asked, over and over. "Is there anything else you need to know?"

Conversation by conversation, she brought her loved ones together. She created the space for them to support her when she needed it most—and, later, for them to support one another, when they needed it most. Death didn't go away, the pain didn't diminish, but the loneliness did. That's what becomes possible when we talk—bravely, awkwardly, openly—about dying and the holes that death leaves behind.

Sex

Sitting in the sterile exam room at a Kaiser hospital in Oakland, a male ob-gyn gives me post-baby intimacy tips. Inside, I burn with mortification, but I refuse to flinch from his steady eye contact.

I'd come to the doctor's office about a year after my first daughter was born to have my Nexplanon contraception implant taken out of my arm, joking that it hadn't been terribly needed in the last few months. I did not expect that offhand remark to lead to a series of follow-up questions from a dude doctor I had just met about the infrequency of sex after giving birth and how I felt about it. But his tone was empathic and respectful. He followed with practical tips, which included words like "schedule" and "reframe intimacy" and "as we age." Oh God, I wanted it to be over, but I did not look away. Partly because I appreciated his effort at directness and partly because he hinted he knew about my podcast, so squirming uncomfortably would've been off-brand.

As I focused my attention on his pupils, I wondered, *How did I become such a cliché? And if I am a cliché, does that mean my sex life is normal? But who wants to be "normal" sexually, especially as a married mom pushing forty?*

The doctor continued, deftly navigating around the land mines about my age, my attractiveness, my *ripeness*. As he sat on a rolling stool in his white coat, he was trying to tell me something comforting and breezy: sex can be fun! It doesn't have to end just one way. That intimacy can be redefined and reset to make room to be playful together. Especially if you want to have another kid, he finally said bluntly. Because transitioning from "rare" or "no sex" to "make-a-baby sex" is a lot of pressure.

I went home and dutifully reported the clear, practical advice to my husband. Arthur and I talked it over in the pragmatic, direct way new parents trade updates about calendar commitments and gaps in childcare. When the conversation was just between us, I didn't need to avert my eyes. Though both of us seemed to ingest the information as "one more thing to add to the to-do list!"

Talking about sex also forced us to be real with each other about the ways parenthood had changed intimacy for us. Our windows of availability had become narrower, more prescribed. Spontaneity was a luxury we did not have. Sex between Arthur and me took on the utility of the seven-minute workout with a hotel desk chair: a little embarrassing, but enough to get the job done. Once, we tried to fit it in before the delivery from the Thai place showed up and barely made it. This was not slow and sexy, but also not *not* fun.

Then, when we decided we wanted to have another baby, several months passed without a positive pregnancy test. I enlisted the help of apps and pee sticks to track my ovulation. I worried about my age and fertility, and whether, like so many of my friends, we'd need to decide how much intervention we were willing to invite. I also was aware that even though we *wanted* another baby, I felt a rush of relief when my period came each month. We had one child and two jobs already. Even though we knew we needed to try now if we ever wanted a second kid, we still exhaled when we got another reprieve.

That conversation with my doctor didn't solve our confusion about timing, but it did make me feel like I had a place to go back to with questions, which I eventually did, about a month before I got pregnant again. It also gave Arthur and me the words that allowed for sex to be more than just for making another baby. In between our very goal-oriented intercourse sessions, we made room for lower-pressure intimacy. I requested more cuddling and "skin-on-skin," the term we'd learned in childbirth classes about newborn attachment. The conversation with my doctor helped me articulate something I needed: a reminder of the physical presence of each other, of the comfort of camaraderie. Especially when so much else was in flux.

Sex is one of the most potent ways we communicate with one another. It's a wordless conversation, but managing its power takes words. Whether it's a onetime fling or a sixty-year marriage, sex requires us to articulate our own needs while attending to someone else's.

I'm defining *sex* broadly here. There is the physical act, but this chapter is about the whole knotty mess that comes with it: our romantic relationships; our bodies; our desires; our wounds; our impulses to attract, dominate, and please others. My focus is on any romantic encounter or relationship where you're navigating what you want, what a partner wants, and what your pairing up requires.

Most often, with a hard conversation about sex, you have a particular audience, someone with whom you've built a connection, and you're trying to ascertain whether each of you wants something more. That's a distinct risk. You are revealing deep, often unspoken desires, so you're risking feeling shame. You're also risking rejection if you want something the other person doesn't. Or, if you're the reluctant one, you're navigating the guilt and discomfort of rejecting someone else.

The best, most open conversations about sex do not pretend these stakes aren't there. In fact, those risks—of shame, abandonment, or hurt—are the starting points. Then you can circle around what you want and need, what the other person wants and needs, and whether those are compatible. While these interactions can be fueled by coy flirtation and physical touch, getting clarity when it comes to sex requires direct conversation. " 'Use your words' is some good advice," sex advice guru Dan Savage has declared. "It's so good, in fact, that I give it all the time."

Of course, the reason we need guides like Dan Savage to give us good advice is because sex and intimacy have always been hard to talk about directly, for reasons that are different from why we avoid talking about other hard topics. Conversations about sex are multilayered and complex, involving our physical selves, our histories of trauma, and our ideas about family, morality, and pleasure.

As so many of our societal mores and conventions surrounding sex are in flux, there's more of an imperative than ever to have these kinds of conversations explicitly. What kind of relationship do you want? How will you treat one another? It used to be that the only socially sanctioned sex existed within a heterosexual marriage. That baggage is definitely still around, but in the last few decades we've seen a vast expansion in what sex and romantic relationships can look like. More unmarried people cohabitate now in America, and more children are living with parents who never bothered with a wedding. Sexual and gender identities are less fixed, and monogamy is not the end goal for many people, especially in younger generations. (Just 43 percent of millennials defined their ideal relationship as "completely monogamous" in a 2020 survey by YouGov.)

At the same time, the pressure on our long-term romantic partnerships has ratcheted up. As relationship therapist Esther Perel has argued, we now expect our spouse to be not just a partner in tending a household, but also a soul mate, a best friend, and an engine for personal growth. "Now we are bringing our need for self-actualization to the marriage," she said to the *New Yorker* in 2018. "We are asking from one person what once an entire village used to provide."

New York Times columnist David Brooks has made the same argument from another angle, mourning what we've lost as our expectations for marriage have become supercharged. "The nuclear family was a mistake," he declared in the *Atlantic* in 2020, a mistake that requires a married, divorced, or never-married couple to bear too much pressure. Fewer Americans live with their extended families now, and fewer live with the support of institutions like unions or churches, which lent stability to many families in post–World War II America. Citing changes in divorce statistics, family size, and marriage rates, he concluded, "When you put everything together, we're likely living through the most rapid change in family structure in human history."

We are expecting each other to fulfill more than ever, at a time when we feel more free to define what love and sex can and should look like in our lives. Drawing up your own romantic model is liberating, but there's also more room for ambivalence and uncertainty. All of us, then, are having to become more skillful at putting words to what we want and need—and to hear and respond to our partner(s) in kind. It's the foundation of consensual sex, and also, what is required of us as we navigate romance, family planning, and long-term expectations.

As a general rule, short sentences can help lead us through that complexity. They allow you to break down our big, complicated feelings into short declarations and opportunities to compare notes. *Do you like this? I want that. Is this okay? Do you want to wait? That feels good. Do you still like this?* Starting these conversations with a new person is intimidating, which is why dating and hooking up can feel terrible. But it's also hard with a long-term partner, because what you need and want from each other can change. Whatever type of intimate relationship you have, these conversations take trust and humility.

Not everyone is worthy of trust. In our sex lives, many of us know the violation of being overpowered, discounted, dismissed, treated as disposable. Sexual assault and abuse happen in many forms. It can be one moment, or a routine, repetitive violation. Some of us are abused as children. Some of us are betrayed by strangers. Some of us, by people we thought were safe. Understanding a sexual violation and its wide-ranging effects takes time, and, hopefully, professional, individualized counseling. You need not rush into disclosing past violations with new partners, nor feel obligated to retell details. Just like with sex, you can decide what you are ready to consent to share. You can say yes or no.

Even when you are talking about sex with someone you trust to be an honest broker, though, there is a degree of risk. You are risking that what you and a partner find out about each other might not be complementary. The answer you discover might be "no thanks." And even if the answer is yes, that just opens up more questions about what you and your partner need in order to feel pleased and safe. You are not going to feel in charge all the time, because someone else gets to decide if they want what you want. But that unsteadiness will always be part of the responsibility of having sex with someone else. You have to step through the awkwardness, say what you expect out of sex together, and admit when that changes.

Talking about sex, and what we might want to do with each other's bodies, is embarrassing. It's tender. And it can also be confusing. Talking about sex can reveal the places where our hearts and minds don't line up. When you notice ambivalence or uncertainty, let me urge you to linger there. It may seem counter-intuitive, or even unsexy, but talking openly about what you don't know—and where you might be curious to explore—gives you and your partner room to breathe. It helps you figure out what you want, and what you might want *together*. And once that's up for discussion, it's simple: the sex is better.

"I don't know yet."

When I was first getting married at twenty-six, a friend of mine who had been married for years wished me "congratulations on a lifelong three-legged race!" I filed it away as a poignant metaphor, one that captured how I wanted my marriage to be: both of us free to propel forward as individuals, but with a new joint core in the middle that we moved together. Four years later, when that marriage was over, I'd look back and realize that a lot of three-legged races end with runners collapsing before reaching the finish line.

When I met Arthur, I still felt like a clump on the ground. I was separated, with divorce papers filed but not finalized. My first husband had moved the last of his things out of our apartment weeks before, the day the New York legislature legalized gay marriage. I was on assignment that night and interviewed people who'd spontaneously gathered at the Stonewall Inn to celebrate. I remember getting a call from my ex telling me he was done moving his boxes out, so I could come home. I told him where I was and joked, "Should I not tell them how hard marriage actually is?"

We could joke by then, because for us, the hardest part of divorce was admitting to each other and to ourselves that we wanted to be apart more than we wanted to stay together. When we finally decided that, I felt a rush of all that could be possible instead. My ex and I had started dating when I was still in college, so I felt like I was stepping out into a charged flow of sexual energy that I'd really never been a part of. I was just getting the hang of that extra beat of eye contact on the subway, at the grocery store, in the bar. I learned to check for a ring. The last time I'd been single, back in college, no one around me had one.

So I definitely noticed Arthur when he showed up from Wyoming at a Fourth of July weekend on Cape Cod hosted by mutual friends, but I was not looking to impress. I proved this, after a long conversation with him on a dock, when I fell into the lake with my too-full cup of gin and tonic. "If you want in on this," I warned him, laughing, "have at it."

After that weekend, he went back to Wyoming, where he was a grad student in ecology, and I returned to New York, but it was clear that we were both excited about each other. We were soon talking on the phone nightly, and then during the day, we sent long emails trying to catch each other up on the lives we'd lived so far: detailed descriptions of our families and our backstories, where we'd lived and why, who in our lives we'd told about the other. Our notes always ended with breathless declarations of how much more we had to talk about.

On my first visit to Laramie, Wyoming, we went to a wedding. Arthur had realized the overlap in dates after I'd excitedly booked my flight, and he offered to skip it, but noted that it'd be a beautiful road trip to get there and a great local band was playing at the reception. I told him I was game, but over email admitted, "I may have a moment of freaked-outness at my first post-divorce nuptials."

He wrote back, "I do hesitate to pull you into that context. But if you tell me whatever you think and feel about it, I bet it will be okay." If I ended up not wanting to go, he offered, we could hang out in the hotel room and I could read trashy celebrity magazines.

On the four-hour drive through central Wyoming, we kept talking, sharing more stories about our families, past relationships, and moments of loneliness. I bought a pack of cigarettes at a gas station, because I was a recent divorcée and I was *just that free*. Where the end of my marriage had at times felt like I was shouting and begging to be heard, here was a man who wanted to know all of me. It gave me swagger.

Driving Wyoming's empty highways under its vast sky, everything felt so open and possible. The wedding was on a mountain hillside, where rows of folding chairs and a few wooden toilet shacks were the only visible signs of human interference. Then the minister began, and as his warm and celebratory welcome slipped into more frequent and rigid quotes from Scripture, I realized he was not taking cues from the expansive landscape. He was Lutheran, and his message centered on commitment and devotion powering a union, with a special emphasis on the wife's duty to hold the family together.

"Love does not make a marriage," I remember him instructing the young couple. "Marriage makes love." In other words, when it sucks, suck it up. That's holy, sacred, and right.

While this was not a worldview I'd ever consciously subscribed to, this minister speaking at the altar was saying all the things I'd told myself over and over in the months before my divorce. Like him, I believed that marriage was a sacred vow, and that my ability to stay committed was a test of whether I really could live my values.

And what were my values around sex and family, and love? I wanted to believe that I was determining those on my own, but the minister was reminding me that my choices, and my shame, drew on hundreds of years of religion and social custom. The hardest part of experiencing my marriage unravel was having to admit that I *could* have a marriage unravel. That I, someone who thought of herself as loyal and devoted to family, might walk away from the most significant and public commitment I'd ever made.

Arthur noticed the ceremony getting to me before I did. I remember a *You okay?* glance as he took my hand when it was over. As we walked back to the truck to drive to the reception, I got light-headed, and, finally, started to cry. Arthur cut off the main trail to separate us from the crowd of guests, and asked if I needed a moment. I didn't, I told him, I was okay. We walked a few more feet, and then under a canopy of evergreens he told me to stop and sit down. He was going to the truck, and I could meet him there.

He walked away, I sat down on a fallen log in my wedding clothes, and finally I let the burning behind my eyes go. I put my face in my hands and released three heaving sobs. I waited to see if there was more, and was surprised to find my body at rest. It was like a sudden wave of nausea, but with hysterical crying. I looked up at the sky through the trees and laughed at the absurdity of my life—all dressed up, sitting on a log, crying about my divorce while this handsome new man waited for me in his truck.

This was supposed to have just been a fun fling, but as I trounced through the pine needles in my dress shoes to get back to him, all of it was feeling bigger. I realized how nice it felt that I'd let myself cry at the party without once wondering if Arthur would be embarrassed, mad, or exasperated. By dropping me off in the woods, he gave me permission to not manage his feelings along with mine. He showed me I didn't have to censor myself to protect him. This was very attractive.

Back at the truck, Arthur was sitting in the driver's seat waiting for me. I opened the passenger side door and found a cluster of purple wildflowers and sagebrush wrapped into a little bouquet. While I cried in the woods alone, he had picked me a bunch of flowers.

Still, as time went on and our early romance turned into a long-distance relationship, and we took turns sorting through our respective worries about what was happening next in our careers, it felt less sexy and too crowded. I was learning how to live by myself for the first time as an adult, still practicing how not to panic and call him or one of my sisters whenever there was a moment of quiet. It was only after my divorce that I realized I didn't know how to be alone with myself. It made me feel childish and pathetic.

And I told him all of this. "I don't know what I'm doing," I would say.

"Just decide if you want to talk to me tomorrow," he'd tell me, remembering later, "That was my refrain for the better part of that year, and the next year." That was comforting to me, because long-term, we made no sense! I was a reporter living in New York and very committed to my career. He was in Wyoming, finishing graduate work in large-mammal ecology.

I could try on different futures while I went about my days in New York, and then I could call him at the end of it. But he was firm on one thing: if we were sleeping together, he didn't want either of us to sleep with anyone else. It felt a little old-fashioned to me, and his clarity on this line frankly surprised me. "If I'm connecting sexually to you, I'm emotionally invested," he told me later. "Obviously, part of it was protecting myself from getting hurt."

Sex, and my desire, were part of my confusion during this time. My physical pull to Arthur was simple, elemental, raw, so in one sense forgoing other partners wasn't a problem. I remember noticing his body in silhouette one morning as he got out of bed, with its sculptural curves and defined muscles, and I wanted to scream, *I'm getting to have sex with* this *man!* It was part of what troubled me as we were falling in love. I worried that I was letting his broad shoulders, deep voice, and the way his jeans hung at his waist seduce me into irresponsible choices.

After my divorce, I needed to know that I could take care of myself on my own. I could feel myself wanting two things equally: Arthur and my freedom. For the next two years, he was okay with me not knowing where we were headed. Then, too much not-knowing caught up with us. I was tired of wondering whether our lives matched up long-term and he was tired of talking me through my ambivalence.

SEX

After some needed time apart, we reconciled. We hadn't resolved all the unknowns about what our relationship and family might look like, but we both firmly knew one thing: we wanted to be with each other. The rest we would figure out together.

In love and sex, so much of what we talk about is chemistry, or *just knowing*. I did not know, and I was afraid because of what I'd gone through before, so I got stuck in cycles of interpreting and reinterpreting what not-knowing must mean.

When Arthur and I were broken up, I realized how precious it was to have a partner I *could* not-know with. I'm so grateful he gave me that freedom, even though revisiting what I had put him through now makes me feel embarrassed and sad. But it was necessary. The space to make the decision to commit to him turned out to be exactly what I needed, so that being with Arthur—and committing to a future together—was a choice I was making and not something that happened to me before I was ready.

"What are you into?"

Of course, not every conversation we have about sex is within a long-term relationship where the question of whether you have a future together looms so large. Plenty of pivotal, high-stakes exchanges happen when you're figuring out what you want to do with someone *right now*.

For sex worker and performer Ty Mitchell, those conversations are part of his job and part of his romantic life. He is used to needing, and getting, different things from sex with different people. He started getting paid for sex work at nineteen, not long after he arrived in New York City for college. Four years

75

later, he started performing in gay porn. When we talked, he was twenty-five years old and in a long-term nonmonogamous relationship with his boyfriend. They both have sex with strangers and friends they connect with online.

So, Ty has had a lot of sex, both professionally and recreationally. He's learned a lot about the range of what can happen during sex, and also what's a constant for him. "There's no such thing as casual sex in the sense there's no feeling, of being able to detach and dissociate. It's not as simple as that, and it's not as clean as that," he told me. "Sex work has taught me a lot about compartmentalizing and its limitations."

Every encounter for him is both emotional and physical. Sometimes, while working on set, he'll feel an intimate connection while the cameras are rolling, and in his personal life he sometimes wants to "get pounded out by a stranger on Grindr." So he makes sure to ask himself and his partners, "What are you into?" It is a prompt that can uncover a lot all at once. The question has its roots in gay cruising culture, a code that immediately moves "the conversation in a certain direction," as Ty said. By asking, you are establishing whether there's mutual interest in a hookup. For him, that creates an opening not just to signal his general preferences, but also what he's in the mood for on that particular day.

Ty has learned to talk quite directly about what he wants and what he expects. Along with his performing and doing sex work for money, he also writes about sex and calls himself "a public intellectual and a public whore." Having so many different kinds of sexual interactions has made Ty realize what all sex has in common. "All sex is power-laden, even if that transaction is 'make me feel better about myself,'" he said in an interview with the gay magazine *Cakeboy* in 2017. When I asked him about that, he added, "The transactional quality to sex work, it creates a power dynamic, but there's usually not equal footing between two people in sex." One of you wants it more, or one of you is more physically dominating. Having one person who is more in charge can be hot, but it also means someone else is *less* in charge. When those roles aren't clearly laid out and agreed to, people can get hurt.

A lot of us navigate this by feel or instinct, but Ty has had the benefit of good instruction. He grew up in Las Vegas, where his mom worked as a cocktail waitress, and as a teenager he hung out with friends who were strippers. All around him was seduction and sex as a commercial exchange. "I didn't really have to work through a lot of shame around it personally," Ty observed.

When Ty arrived in New York to start at NYU, his best friend at the time was a sex worker about two years older, whom Ty now calls his "model for casual sex." Ty liked the way he talked about hookups, that they weren't about anonymous, emotionally numb orgasms, but simply another way to connect, even if they were very temporary interactions. His friend taught him the term *transactional sex*, a concept reclaimed by sex work advocates. Money could be part of the "transaction" of sex, Ty came to believe, and it could simultaneously be a consensual, enjoyable, and honest experience. "That made it feel a lot more accessible to me," Ty said. And, he realized, every kind of sex is a transaction. So you have to be clear about the terms each time.

For example, before Ty performs and has sex on camera, his contract is set up by agents and stipulates exactly what he does and doesn't want to do. When he's booking a one-on-one appointment with someone who wants to pay him to meet up, the initial negotiations start out more vaguely. "I have to be discreet, especially because I'm working on text and calls," he said. But when he meets a paying client in person, he is clear and up-front about what is going to happen. Even when things get hot, he's learned it's best to be consistent and certain about where the exchange is going to end. Sometimes that requires the declaration: "No, it's just not available."

The word *transactional* can sound cold and mercenary, like a backroom political deal. But Ty's point is that any consensual sexual relationship is a kind of exchange. Despite what sex columnists and movie scenes would have us believe, sex is not always going to be a one-for-one (or more) orgasm pleasure fest between two people. In a long-term monogamous relationship, for example, one partner may have sex because the other person is in the mood, or, as I wrote about earlier, because one of you is ovulating and the other has the sperm. Or one person may be looking for an adventurous night of experimentation, and the other hopes for the possibility of something deeper, and at least a follow-up call. When people decide to have sex together, their reasons may complement each other, but they don't necessarily have to be coming together for the same reason. Sex work, when one person is getting pleasure and the other is getting money, just makes that exchange more plain.

Ty's work has clarified the terms of any relationship he gets in. Traditional monogamy is not a possibility, nor is a relationship where he has to always be up for sex. Sometimes, "I'm beat because of work. My sex drive feels really depleted," he recognized. With his long-term partner, it's other qualities, like everyday companionship and a shared history together, that form the foundation of their relationship.

Still, he told me, even after years together, their sex is very hot. They each know what the other likes, and they trust each other "to go places maybe you're not as secure." Allowing that they individually don't need to satisfy all of each other's sexual needs has lowered the pressure for when they do have sex. "I have sex with him in a way I don't with other people," Ty told me. "It's the most consistently fulfilling sexually of any relationship I've been in."

All our sex lives should start with the question, "What are you into?" That prompts an investigation into your particular desires and turnoffs. That exploration can start on your own, alone with your own hands, maybe with porn. Then, when you move out of the realm of fantasy into the fleshy, clumsy encounters in real life, you've got to ask yourself what you're into all over again. It might be the same as what you like in your fantasies, it might be different, and it might change.

You'll also have to tell someone else what you're into, and ask that of them. This kind of conversation with a partner—whether new or long-term—is about more than asking for or granting consent. That's essential, but it's just the start. You also have to be direct and honest about what you want and expect from intimacy with each other. That's much more difficult to articulate. There are plenty of reasons to try to skip the conversation and pretend you want the same thing in order to minimize conflict, but there are no right words to make that negotiation go away. The negotiation is happening. It's at the heart of sex, this multi-layered dance of flirtation, seduction, and release. We're trying to signal what we want from someone while simultaneously trying to read what they want from us. As awkward as it can be, "What are you into?" is a direct route to finding out what you both want from each other. Like any transaction, that requires figuring out, and saying out loud, what you need and expect.

"I'm sorry I hurt you."

Questioning the confines of monogamy, as Ty does, is different from cheating. Cheating involves betrayal and dishonesty, not just having sex with someone else. And often, people cheat less to seek novelty and more to blow everything up. Flirting and falling into bed with someone else is a lot easier than summoning the courage to tell your partner that you want out, or you feel abandoned, or you feel numb and you don't know why. Sometimes infidelity is the exclamation point that ends a relationship. Sometimes it is the first line in a much-needed conversation.

Some couples do survive these ruptures. Paul and Megan, for example, made the choice to get married even after he'd confessed to a long pattern of affairs and illicit meetups. Megan responded when I was casting about for couples who had been through affairs, because I was curious to see what conversations kept them invested in their relationship after the hurt of betrayal.

Megan does not downplay the horror of her experience. "Thirty days before my wedding I found out my fiancé was a full-blown sex addict," she wrote in the first email she sent to me. But she can retell the story with a remarkable absence of animus toward Paul, in large part because they've kept talking about it together. To my surprise, after I spoke to Megan, Paul volunteered to tell me more details, "because talking to you was helpful for Megan."

When Paul started hooking up with other women, he told himself he deserved it. He'd been dating Megan for about five years and they'd bought a house together, but their mismatched libidos had started to grate on him. He was angry. He thought about sex all the time and could feel its charge in the air from even glancing at an attractive woman at a stoplight. "My mind goes to if she would like me and would think I'm attractive. I wonder what our life will be like together. I wonder if she's into things that I am," he told me. "And it all happens in a matter of seconds."

Then he'd come home and want to have sex, and often Megan didn't feel like it. To her, she told me, it felt like his sexual needs were insatiable, and that was tiresome. Paul first turned to porn—Megan knew he watched a lot of it and was fine with his habit—but over time, seeing the same camera shots started to mute its thrill. That's when Paul told me he started looking at Craigslist Casual Encounters. Initially it was just to read the ads, to fantasize about the people in his seemingly quiet, conservative town offering these salacious posts. He'd pull up the site at work, where he had a cubicle in a big corporate office. Sometimes he would take his phone to the bathroom to watch porn and masturbate "multiple times a day, every day," he admitted to me. "I honestly don't know how I didn't lose my job. I would disappear from my desk and I would be gone sometimes for over an hour."

He was giving himself permission to indulge, sneaking around and not getting caught, and that eventually led to answering and posting ads on Craigslist himself. He would meet up with women, sometimes to have sex, or when he wasn't sure he could perform physically, he still liked to get together to talk about sexual fantasies. "I was always trying to find someone who I felt was sort of on that same level and could speak that language with me."

When Paul was having these clandestine meetups, Megan was at home planning their wedding, thinking Paul was out playing hockey or getting beers. One night, when he didn't come home until after four in the morning, Megan remembered, "He said, 'I'm sorry. I had too much to drink and fell asleep in the car.'" Megan believed him.

Then a woman Paul met through Craigslist told him she didn't want to see him anymore, and in a desperate plea he now sees as pitiable, he asked her if she knew anyone else who might want to meet up with him. She gave him a name and a phone number, and Paul texted the number. He now thinks it was some sort of prank, because the other woman's husband was soon texting him back, angrily trying to guess who was propositioning his wife. Paul realized he'd tossed a grenade into a stranger's marriage and was out of control.

He decided to confess. Paul had proposed to Megan, he told me, because he knew he wanted to be with Megan for the rest of his life. He never doubted that. But finally he realized all his lying was putting everything at risk. "My thought process was, sooner or later I'm not going to be able to deal with the guilt of knowing these things that she doesn't know. And so, if I'm ultimately going to break down and tell her, it's probably better for me to tell her now as opposed to, you know, two years into our marriage." And so, he told her.

"On the day of my bridal shower," Megan told me.

He confessed everything: the consuming porn use, the Craigslist meetups, all the women he'd slept with, some of whom Megan knew. "It was very much just kind of vomiting up all these stories that I had," Paul said.

Megan felt humiliated and stupid, but she now had crucial information that had been missing. She'd noticed Paul withdrawing and didn't know why and wondered what she had been doing wrong. "It was chaos in my brain. I couldn't figure out how to reignite things," she said. "I remember one night, we got into it about what we were going to have for dinner. I left the house to go to the store to get exactly what he wanted. I told him, 'If that is what you want, I'll go do it, just quit being a weirdo.' That's an argument that stuck in my head."

Now at least she felt like she had an answer. "I just said, 'Okay.' I don't know if it was the shock, but I said, 'Thank God we're finally dealing with it.' I really was like, this makes sense." Paul's apology at the center of his confession was central; he did not excuse his behavior or downplay the hurt he'd caused. That's what gave them room to also talk about whether their relationship was worth saving.

"Fear of loss rekindles desire, makes people have conversations they haven't had in years, takes them out of their contrived illusion of safety," Esther Perel has said of recovering from infidelity. That's what happened for Paul and Megan. After Paul's confession, he and Megan took sick days from work the next three days as they talked and cried together. He told her about the deep shame of his secrets, of realizing how much he'd compartmentalized his compulsions and totally disregarded her. He wanted to come completely clean, and his admissions stretched out over days as he remembered details. "Finally, she said, 'I'm at my limit. If you remember anything else, I don't want to know about it,'" Paul said.

Megan listened, but she wasn't always calm or understanding. "The gravity of the anonymous Craigslist encounters hit me, and I lost my shit. We were driving down the highway and I was hitting him," Megan told me. "This made it sink in for me that this guy's out of control, instead of, like, a dirtbag. I felt bad for him." Paul felt that pity, which made him wonder why Megan would consider staying with him. "There's a part of me that's always going to wonder if it was a saving-face kind of thing." Did she really want to be alongside him while he dealt with all this, or was it just "less embarrassing than having to explain it to everyone she knows that the wedding's off because Paul's a piece of shit and couldn't keep it in his pants?"

But Megan said this rupture helped her too. She looked back and saw all the ways she'd tried to contain conflict and please Paul. Now she got to renegotiate the terms of their relationship as he asked for her forgiveness. "I had never been a person who was good at asking for what I want," she told me. "I can ask for what I want now. We're open with how we talk. It had never been like that."

Megan is much quicker now to point out to Paul when he's not managing his stress well, or withdrawing, or picking fights with her unfairly. "I've definitely gained some strange confidence because I just feel like I can say things a little more freely now. Like, you put me through hell and back, I'm going to tell you what's wrong with you," she said.

Paul started confronting his behaviors, which he now admitted were not Megan's fault. They started researching sex addiction together, and for Paul, the descriptions felt very familiar. Megan went with him to his first recovery meeting. Talking with others and hearing their stories helped him better understand his problem and shattered his illusion that what he was doing on the side didn't affect anyone else. He considered the long-term consequences of his actions: being with Megan was important to him, and Megan did not want him to be with someone else, so he had to change. Or, as a phrase he learned in meetings put it, "Okay. I have a problem. If I act out, I'm going to have two."

Paul started going to recovery meetings regularly, where he got support and guidance as he tried to build back a healthy sex life with Megan. First, he gave up sex completely. Then, he and Megan settled into having sex about once a week, with Paul experimenting with whether he could watch porn without spiraling out of control. But he doesn't indulge certain old behaviors. "I cannot go on Craigslist anymore. I cannot have sex with women who are not my wife anymore," Paul told me. And they've adopted other rules, like Megan can look at Paul's phone and computer whenever she wants.

They both made a choice after Paul's disclosure and apology. Paul took responsibility without first having to get caught. Megan listened and ultimately decided she wanted to try to help him as she held him accountable for the hurt he had caused. They decided to make choices to serve something bigger: the future they've committed to together.

"Someone hurt me."

Not everyone who experiences a violation, though, gets to tend to that wound with the person who caused it. That's not always safe, and, frankly, it might be something you don't want to do. When someone hurts you, whether through emotional betrayal or physical abuse or assault, you do not owe them a resolution. But you do carry the impacts of what they did. And it's up to you to figure out how to tell the story of what happened.

A woman named Karla told me about when she was sexually assaulted in college. We talked years after her assault, and she said she has learned it helps to blurt out what she *does* want when it comes to sex. With her boyfriend Manny, whom she started dating a few years after her assault, she told me, "Both of us like it kind of rough." After sex, they debrief on their pillows, talking over what clicked and what didn't this time around. It's playful, safe, declarative.

What she remembers about her assault is her immediate lack of clarity. Karla had gone out with a big group of friends to a series of bars to celebrate the end of the semester while her roommate stayed back to study for one last final. Karla wasn't alarmed at first when their group thinned as the night went on, but then it was just her and her roommate's boyfriend walking back late to the apartment. He started drunkenly talking about her body, describing how he found her attractive. Then, when they were walking past a church, he told her to look away, and clumsily landed a sloppy kiss on her.

"I was just like, 'What the fuck?'" she said, and put her hand up to dismiss what felt like a dumb, drunken move. "I still didn't find it a dangerous situation." Then she noticed how he was backing her into a corner of the railing at the church's entrance, and realized she was pinned in. "That's when he shoved his tongue down my throat. It got more and more repetitive. He did it a couple of times, and I could not move from that corner. I kept trying and I couldn't," she recalled. She kept resisting, telling him no, to get off, that he was with her roommate. She could see other people walking by in the dark. "No one stopped."

When it was over, she said, "I still had to walk home with him after that. He offered to buy me McDonald's. I declined." Once they got to the apartment, he slept in a bed next to Karla's, with his arms around her roommate. When Karla woke up and saw him across the room, she hurried to the bathroom, where she remembers her hands were shaking so much she couldn't buckle her belt. "I had this pit of dread in my stomach. I felt very nauseous. I couldn't really see straight," she told me. "I knew something was wrong because my body was not right."

Karla didn't know how to put words to what had happened, to parse responsibility and blame, and sort where, on the hierarchy of violation, her experience fell. Through one lens, it was just a kiss. Through another, she'd been trapped, overpowered, and ignored. "The thing that was the most difficult was that it wasn't rape, and I was reacting this way." She waited until her roommate's finals were over before telling her what had happened. Her roommate, a friend from home whom she'd been close to for years, dismissed it. "She blamed me, alcohol, anyone but him."

Within a few weeks, after the start of the next semester, Karla's roommate moved out. She never returned her keys, but stopped paying rent, leaving Karla thousands of dollars short.

Karla felt alone and embarrassed. She had never even had sex and now she had to tell her conservative Guatemalan parents why she needed extra money to cover her rent. "They were very, very sad about it," Karla said. Her father had to borrow money from an uncle and some friends to help out. She also told some of her close friends what had happened—and asked those with boyfriends to never leave her alone with them.

Her body didn't forget. "I would hear keys jingling down the hallway and freeze, staring at the door until the sound stopped. I would have nightmares of him coming over, banging on the door to no end." She started wearing baggy clothes and cut all her hair off because she didn't want to attract men's attention. When she had sex for the first time about a year after she was assaulted, "I kept wanting to cover up parts of my body," she said. Still, she didn't mind getting physical with someone—she just didn't want anything serious. "Sex was easy, but emotions were not."

When Karla met Manny, she had no intention of ever telling him about that night, what she'd come to refer to as "my assault." Then, after two months of seeing each other, Karla was with him when she heard from mutual friends that her former roommate had gotten engaged to her boyfriend. Karla felt that familiar panic spread over her body. "It felt like a wave of hopelessness, because I had just felt so small." She couldn't sleep that night, as she cried and replayed the whole experience in her head. The next day, she told Manny she wasn't feeling well and he offered to take her to get ice cream. "I really couldn't hold in my emotions about it," she remembered, and started explaining to him why she was upset, that an old friend was marrying a really terrible guy.

Finally, she just told the story: "Walking home, how he cornered me, that it wasn't rape, but it was still a violation." She told him that she'd been hurt and that it had lasting effects she doesn't always understand.

That conversation opened up the way they communicated, and the way they had sex. Manny told her that he could tell she was detached and aloof during sex, just going along with it, and this allowed them to talk about how to have sex that felt safe and fun together. "We definitely had to go through stages of what he can't do and why he can't do it," Karla said. "One time he held me down and I was just like, 'Wait, no, no, no,' and we just completely stopped because it was something that I didn't like at all."

Lying together after sex, and putting into words how her body felt and hearing how his felt, have unlocked a kind of directness she'd never had before with a man. Manny encouraged her to go back to therapy to talk more about what had happened and how she was trying to protect herself. She's also a lot less reticent now to acknowledge a conflict in their relationship, something she used to avoid because she had been afraid he'd reject her, particularly after having both a man overpower her and her close friend not believe and then abandon her.

"Communication made me less afraid that he would leave," Karla said. "It's like you're saying, *I want to continue to make this work and therefore I'm bringing this up*." Telling Manny about the assault made her feel exposed and foolish all over again, but she ultimately learned that it was the opposite of her assault. Here, she was giving voice to the tender parts of herself, and having them heard, rather than having them dismissed.

It was also practice for the conversations they've continued to have about intimacy and their relationship. Whether or not there's a history of assault, most of us bring previous hurts into romantic relationships. When we are trying to be attractive to someone and lean into the thrill of new romance, the impulse to try to wall off past shames is understandable. You don't have to describe the details of how it happened, but you also don't have to hide that someone has hurt you. When you are ready to share, disclosing to a new partner can create closeness. That openness gives you a foundation to build on together.

"I'm really sad this didn't work out."

Karla's hurt was caused by an assault, by being overpowered without her consent. That she was saying no didn't matter; her assaulter just kept pushing and pushing. Hearing her objections would have meant not getting what he wanted in that moment. It would've meant hearing her rejection and honoring it.

Learning to accept rejection is equally as important as learning how to clearly give and ask for permission. "Rejection needs to be normalized, not catastrophized," Suzanne Degges-White, a professor of counseling at Northern Illinois University, told the *Huffington Post* in 2018. "No one likes being passed over, but it's going to happen more times in life than we like to imagine."

Passing on a partner, or being passed on, is a routine part of dating. You might argue it's the *point* of dating—winnowing through the options. Finding the right person usually comes with unrequited love, lust, and crushes in the meantime. Sometimes a partner leaves without explanation, or a date or flirtation just ends mysteriously. Even if you can manage to handle a breakup conversation with grace, there is no graceful way to trudge through the hurt of not being picked or desired, or loved enough for someone to put in more effort.

Our cultural love stories lack models for accepting rejection. Instead, trying to reverse a rejection is the fuel that powers a lot of romantic comedies. Julie Beck wrote in the *Atlantic* about a study that found watching these movies actually made women more tolerant of stalking behavior, and cited an *Onion* headline: "Romantic-Comedy Behavior Gets Real-Life Man Arrested."

"Begging for sex or a relationship despite a woman's expressed wishes is a beloved staple of pop culture," writer Cord Jefferson observed in the *Guardian* in 2014, in a piece where he described his own devastating breakup that he couldn't accept. "I got the message—but not before I'd convinced myself that it was her fault I'd been behaving like a maniac stalker."

That breakup was years ago, and I reached out to Cord to hear more about how he thought he'd mishandled it. He told me this was his first love, a woman he met at twenty-three and assumed he'd marry. They had started dating when she was still in college and he was just out. They moved to New York together, then continued their relationship when she moved back to California to be near family while he struggled to launch a writing career after the financial crisis. He finally got a job at a Washington think tank, but it wasn't the kind of work he really wanted to do, and he was starting to feel left behind as other college friends were joining law practices and making real money.

At least he had his girlfriend, he'd told himself a lot during those first months in Washington.

Then she broke it off on New Year's Eve in 2009, when she called Cord from the airport. They'd been together for almost five years at that point, long-distance for the last two, and rather than get on that plane to come see him, she was calling to tell him she couldn't do it—the trip, the relationship, any of it. Cord begged her to just get on the plane so they could talk in person. He felt like she owed him that much. But she didn't relent.

Their phone call lasted less than ten minutes. After she hung up, she never discussed the breakup with him again. It was over.

Cord told only his parents about the breakup. "I was embarrassed. I was ashamed that she had broken up with me," he said. After, Cord went out a lot, drank a lot, smoked a lot. His friends, the ones that felt a few steps ahead of him in adulthood, didn't notice.

In private, he kept reaching out to his ex. He couldn't shake the feeling that he could do more to win her back. He sent her repeated emails, called and left messages, sent flowers, and wrote her a long, handwritten letter. She didn't respond to any of it. "I got angry," he said. "I felt like she robbed me of closure."

Rage was a common emotional reaction at the time for Cord. He'd actually started going to therapy a few months before the breakup, looking for help managing his anger. He wasn't prone to violence, but when frustrated or insulted he had a habit of totally shutting down. He remembered one night when they were still dating, walking around New York, looking for a place to eat. His girlfriend stepped up to a restaurant window to look at the menu and quickly dismissed it as out of their price range. Cord got irritated about the casual way she declared it inaccessible to them, even though she was right that they couldn't afford it. "It made me feel so lame and childish and pathetic and so weak, but rather than telling her that, I got super cold and standoffish," he recalls. "I was just mean to her for the rest of the night."

He knew he was being an asshole. Inside, he was asking himself why he couldn't let it go, but he was encased in his anger and didn't try to explain himself or apologize. "I wasn't a very good boyfriend. I don't think I was very open or honest, or particularly kind," he admitted. "I felt like I wasn't bringing much to the table as a partner and I was insecure about that, but I don't think I would've risked being vulnerable in that way."

Cord finally talked more about the breakup in therapy. "I didn't want to appear not masculine if I was sad or crying," he said, but he worked through that. And with the help of his psychologist he learned, when he feels rage, to pause to think through what is causing it. "Now I'm a lot more willing to admit when I'm afraid or I'm hurt."

It was a different heartbreak that led to that shift for him. Cord's mother found a lump in her breast in 2013. Her cancer didn't respond to treatment, leaving him feeling helpless, angry, and victimized by forces he couldn't wrestle back. This time, though, there was no one he could try to convince to undo it. When his mother died in 2016, he had no one to email to make his case, no one to beg that it didn't have to end this way. "One of the things it crystallized was, [my mom's death] was a million times harder than my breakup, and I got through it." He did so by taking care of himself: he wrote more, quit smoking, ate healthier, and started working out. "And I came out on the other side of that still feeling sad and a sense of loss, but not ashamed of myself and not beating myself up all the time."

It gave him a new word to understand why he had such a difficult time accepting that his girlfriend wanted to move on without him: *grief*. "I'd fallen in love with this relationship over the course of four and a half years and it had become the most important thing in the world to me, and it was gone," he said.

He was still really sad their relationship was over. It had given his life some shape when he felt uncertain about most everything else. But he never told her that. Instead, he blamed his girlfriend for taking their relationship away from him. More than ten years later, he can see why she stopped putting up with him, and why, once she had decided, she didn't want to give him an opportunity to talk her out of it. "I was probably incapable of accepting what she would say," he explained. At the time, he felt "like the one good thing that was left in my life was her, so I probably would've said anything and been deaf to anything that she said."

When you're rejected, it's not the other person's job to take that sting away. More information can help cobble together a narrative, but that kind of conversation requires that both people feel like they'll be listened to. That wasn't the case in Cord's breakup. Sometimes it's a courtesy to tell the person you're leaving what had happened, so they have some thread to go on, but sometimes it just needs to be said and left at that. Particularly, Cord knows, for women rejecting a certain kind of man, the sort he was when he was twenty-seven. "It should go without saying that women aren't carnival prizes to be won. But just like with lots of things that should go without saying, it needs to be said," Cord wrote in that *Guardian* article four and a half years after that breakup. "A hurt man can be a handful—but a hurt man inspired by the conviction that he's owed something can be dangerous."

"What I want has changed."

It is painful to absorb rejection, as Cord and most any of us have felt at some point. Doing the rejecting can also be difficult, because it requires that you look at someone who wants to be with you, and saying you don't agree. Coyly brushing off an overeager stranger at a bar can be awkward; deciding to leave a relationship you've committed to can be excruciating. That means telling someone you've loved: *I know this will hurt you, but what I want has changed*.

It takes time to gather the nerve to do that. It also takes time to determine what trade-offs you can tolerate in an intimate relationship, and what are deal-breakers. Those calculations can change over time. Just as I needed time to tell Arthur, "I don't know," when we were sorting through our future together, long-term breakups usually take shape first in internal monologues before the direct conversation can happen with someone else.

Actor Jane Fonda told me on *Death, Sex & Money* about her thought process as she was deciding to divorce Ted Turner:

> I knew that if I stayed with him, I could never be a fully realized person, and I had to make a decision and it was really scary. I felt like Virginia Woolf, only I had two angels in the house.

One on one shoulder saying, "Oh come on, Fonda. Lighten up! The guy's got two million acres of the most gorgeous land in the world and he's funny and he keeps you laughing!" And on the other shoulder, there was an angel with a very soft whisper saying, "Jane, you can stay with him and die married, but you'll die not being whole." And so I opted for the whisper.

After Fonda filed for divorce, she moved into her daughter's spare bedroom in Atlanta, "a room with no closet." She told me it was a time of "tremendous pain and sadness that the marriage hadn't worked," but alongside that, she noticed the beginnings of the confidence that, for the first time in her life, she could be okay without a man by her side.

Ellen Allen heard a similar whisper that she needed a change. When it first came to her, she would go *into* her closet. That's where she kept her well-worn copy of the book *My Secret Garden*, in the home she shared with her husband and teenage daughter. *My Secret Garden*, written in 1973 by Nancy Friday, is a collection of mostly anonymous women's sexual fantasies. Ellen had started reading it in her thirties, and she reread one particular lesbian sex scene so often the spine on the book broke. "It would just flop open right to it," she said with a laugh.

When I met Ellen, she was just beginning to reset her life, going on dates with women but still sharing a house with her husband and daughter, though I didn't know that at the time. Ellen has long worked in social service advocacy in my home state of West Virginia, and she was an important source for me when I was just starting out in journalism. When I interviewed her years later for this book, after she'd moved out of the house and gotten a divorce, she told me that, while she'd known she was attracted to women since she was young, she decided when she was a teenager that being out was simply not a possibility for her. She was raised a Southern Baptist in a small town in southern West Virginia. Ellen was the youngest of three children in her family, and by the time she was a teenager she was the only living child. One brother died at age seven during routine surgery when Ellen was three. Then her oldest brother was killed by a drunk driver just after he finished high school when Ellen was thirteen. "I vowed then I would do everything in my power to make my parents happy," she told me. "I made the decision, and I didn't revisit it until my forties."

Ellen met her husband when she was a teenager and he was officiating a softball game she was playing in. They married when she was twenty-four and he was twenty-eight, and they had a daughter, Sara, who was blind at birth due to a congenital condition. Ellen and her husband both desperately love their daughter and helped manage her health care and schooling. It was a busy, full life, Ellen said. "I just learned to adapt and created a life that was good enough, until it wasn't any longer."

It started when Ellen and another married mom in town admitted to each other, tentatively at first, that they both felt attracted to women. They knew everything this opened up, how explosive it could be for their families and their place in their conservative town, so at first it was easier to write than say anything out loud. They started exchanging letters that described how they felt about women and, eventually, with more specificity, how they felt about each other.

They wrote back and forth, giving Ellen a place to put words to that whisper she'd never said out loud, and they each explored all the consequences of giving in to what they wanted. Neither had been with a woman before. Discussing the possibility of being together, over what Ellen said was more than a dozen hand-delivered letters, was exhilarating and dangerous-feeling. "It was very tumultuous because we were torn about our families, and knowing we were doing something deceptive."

She began a secret physical affair with the married woman that lasted three years. The woman Ellen was with did not identify as a lesbian, "and that way it was kind of safe because I didn't have to make a decision." But Ellen's sexuality was never a question for her, which she finally admitted to the married woman. "It was like, *Oh wow, did I say that out loud?*" she said, thinking of the half a lifetime that had passed before she could say it. "It's really amazing what we're capable of," Ellen told me. "I'm clearly a lesbian!"

She'd always had in her mind that once her daughter was grown she could come out and live as a lesbian in her sixties. But now, in her mid-forties, this was happening, while she was still married, and the lying weighed on her. "It wreaked havoc on my nervous system," she said, "being fragmented continually."

It took time for the truth to come out. "I recall much uncertainty about whether I would ever gather the courage to change my life." Two years into her affair, Ellen told her secret girlfriend that she had to tell her husband about their relationship. The woman felt uncomfortable, but Ellen's husband responded more openly. Ellen told him she'd long known she was attracted to women and she needed to explore this part of herself, "and he was okay with that, but I don't think he understood—and perhaps I didn't either at the time—the depths of who I was." He joined some of her therapy sessions, and together they developed a plan for co-parenting and reorganizing their family.

The term she and her husband used to describe the arrangement was *parallel lives*, something they learned from a book they got in counseling. They agreed on a structure where Ellen could explore what she wanted, but they'd keep their family together without making any permanent decisions about their relationship. And they would wait four years to tell their daughter. When Ellen's lover eventually broke off their affair, Ellen was heartbroken. "It was a relationship of respect and we cared about one another," she said. "It just couldn't work any longer." But she was also unable to go back to how things had been before the relationship.

Ellen and her husband were coping quietly, trying to see what could still hold in the midst of all the change. "He was pretty sure that this would pass and we could coexist." Ellen remembers one particular conversation where he tried to make it all work. "I'll never forget this, because he's a very quiet man. He looked at me and said, 'Ellen, I don't care what you do. Just don't leave us,'" her voice catching as she recalled this. "It probably kept me there longer. If there was any anger ever at all, it was, 'I didn't leave my daughter. I left you.'"

Ellen took a job about an hour away, but was home every other day to pick up their daughter. Even as she started going on dates with women, she didn't feel an urgency to file for divorce, which would also mean admitting to their friends and community why Ellen was leaving.

Then Ellen met Sue.

"Sue just knocked me totally off my feet," Ellen said. They both worked in advocacy around intimate partner violence, including in the LGBTQ+ community. Sue was out, and almost immediately Ellen came out to her and explained her living arrangement, that it bought her and her husband time to keep their family together while Ellen explored what could be next. As Ellen got to know Sue, she saw a vision of what could be, and only a few months later Ellen "just told her that I was attracted to her and I'd like to spend more time with her." But Sue didn't want to get involved until Ellen had made some decisions. "Until we had formalized our separation and started our divorce, there was only bike riding."

Ellen felt even more pulled apart trying to live two lives at once, which pushed her to finally end her marriage. "I couldn't be with her in the way I wanted to. It was really stressful," Ellen realized. She had to do two things she'd always wanted to avoid: tell her mother and tell her daughter.

Ellen's father had died by this time. She still vividly remembers the physical sensation of panic as she drove to her mother's house to come out to her. "It did not go well." Her mother gave Ellen a book from her pastor. "It was called *When Homosexuality Hits Home*, and it was beyond offensive. She's sure I'm going to hell." More than a decade later, they don't discuss Ellen's love life, even after Ellen married Sue in 2013. "She still hasn't met Sue, refuses to," Ellen said. But Ellen dutifully visits a couple of times a month, driving the two hours south to her mother's home alone. "I have a relationship with her because I choose to, but it's all on her terms. I'm an only child and she needs me."

After Ellen and her husband agreed to tell their daughter their marriage was over, Ellen told her daughter, who was fifteen at the time, about her sexuality. "He made me do it by myself," Ellen remembered. "I told her we were getting a divorce because I'd come out of the closet as a lesbian and I could no longer live, knowing that, with her father." Then her husband went in to talk to their daughter and closed the door. "I still don't know what he said."

She thinks back on that difficult, tumultuous time now as proof that she can be brave. About a year after everything had been revealed, Ellen said that her daughter just offhandedly observed, "Mom, you're so much happier!" Ellen told me, "And to hear that from your daughter, it's affirming. Intellectually you know you're doing the right thing, but to have that affirmed by someone you just love, it was something I'll never forget."

Everything that Ellen had long feared about coming out—rejection, scorn, and ostracization from her community—all happened. Her mother cannot accept whom Ellen loves. Ellen became a community scandal, and some of her lifelong friends stopped speaking to her. Some talked to her daughter to express concern behind Ellen's back. She sees now that there was no way she could've stayed in her town, where she'd lived all her life, as an out lesbian.

Coming out didn't resolve all the conflicts and tensions in Ellen's life. There are plenty of uncomfortable things to navigate together with Sue. They've had to figure out how to define Sue's role with Ellen's daughter—they're very close but have chosen not to use the word *stepmother*—and how to handle the tension when Ellen goes back and forth to her mother's, where Sue's existence is unacknowledged.

But Ellen knows now that loving someone does not mean always being able to protect them from hurt. Though admitting she wanted something different was terrifying at first, by slowly and incrementally talking about it, and being honest about the costs that came with all the changes, she finally could stop hiding.

"The exhilaration was always there. Even going through a divorce, as difficult as they can be, every single day I felt a new freedom," she told me. "It's like going down a long, steep hill on smooth pavement. You can feel the wind in your hair. You can feel the energy. You just feel like you're twelve years old."

"My body is different now."

For Ellen, claiming her sexual identity was about declaring a secret, one that was long-held but always clear to her. For her, making this change was a matter of courage, not overcoming uncertainty. She knew what she wanted.

Our sexual desires are not always so clear, and often they are a moving target. The sorts of relationships we have and the kinds of sex we want vary by life phase. "I learned you could have dozens of sexual awakenings, each one different than the last," Carmen Maria Machado wrote in the *Los Angeles Review of Books* in 2015. "Every time, I learned something new about my body, about who I was. I felt like I was making up for lost time."

Sometimes newly emerging desires push our bodies into different phases. Other times our bodies are the ones doing the pushing and forcing change against our will. Antidepressants can do this, by messing with our libidos. So can getting older. Or getting sick.

Traci Smith was forty-four and a single mom when she was diagnosed with breast cancer. Traci's mother was diagnosed thirty years before her, and they had never talked about it. "She didn't want to make a big deal of it," Traci remembered. "She just didn't want to bother anyone." Traci had that same impulse, initially. She first noticed the lump under her arm about six months before she asked a doctor about it. Then, she learned the statistics about higher mortality from breast cancer for Black women, despite their slightly lower incidence rates compared to non-Hispanic white women, because of delayed diagnosis and less access to high-quality medical care. So Traci decided she would "talk about it, so it's not a disease you have to fight behind closed doors."

Over four years, Traci would eventually get a mastectomy, radiation, a preventative mastectomy on the other side, and reconstructive plastic surgery. But it all started with six months of chemotherapy. At her chemo clinic in Philadelphia, she always arrived dressed up, and often brought a gaggle of supporters along with her. "Although I was sick, I made it a point not to look sick." That meant wearing the best wigs and eyelashes for her chemo appointments. Often, she said, doctors and nurses would think she was a visitor rather than a patient when she showed up for treatment. During what she came to call her "chemo parties," her daughter, her daughter's father, and groups of friends would come and gather while she got her infusions. She would nod on and off in the midst of their conversations because the chemo made her sleepy.

Traci noticed the other patients, particularly women, who were alone and down as they got their treatments. She wondered what she could do for them and thought of her hairstylist, who was one of the first people Traci told about her diagnosis. She proposed a day of beauty at the salon for these other women patients—and they did it. Thirteen women going through chemo were paired up with a personal stylist and a makeup artist. "I got a limo and picked them up," she said. "Because a lot of your healing is mental healing."

That led to monthly workshops and support gatherings, Mother's Day brunches, and Ladies' Nights through a nonprofit Traci started, called Traci's BIO (Beautiful Inside & Out).

Her group expanded to serve other Black women, whom she connected with through mutual friends and Facebook.

As they celebrated each other, Traci found that her fellow patients wanted to talk about the indignities of cancer: the surgery that transformed the ways their bodies looked; the hair loss and the bad breath; the brittle fingernails and toenails; the drop in libido; "this horrible discharge" and other hormonal changes that made them feel even more like strangers in their bodies. "When you have chemo, although it cures you, it's just a horrible, horrible way for the cancer to leave your body," she told me. "So we talked about it."

Before cancer, this was not the way Traci operated socially. She'd always been a private person, one much more comfortable grinding through work away from the spotlight. ("I was vice president of my class, not president, for seventh, eighth, ninth, tenth, eleventh, and twelfth grades," she said, laughing.) But she was motivated to talk honestly about the trade-offs of cancer treatment to underscore for herself and other women why the costs were worth it. "The number one thing I talk about is survivorship. You have to do whatever it takes to fight and survive," she said. "Once you're surviving, let's talk about everything else."

Traci was the moderator, event planner, and counselor in these conversations. She coached her fellow patients as they mourned the bodies they'd had before cancer, and confided to her how their intimate partners supported them, or rejected them, in the aftermath.

Traci had never married, and as she talked other women through all these changes, she was not having sex with anyone. She just wasn't interested as she went through her own treatment.

"The last thing you're thinking about is being intimate," she said. "I have one boob, I have no hair, and I am not feeling myself at all." And then, to Traci's surprise, she started dating someone new a few months after her last reconstructive surgery.

She'd known this guy for a while. He was a caterer in town, who'd handled a family baby shower, and then her mother's funeral, and then a community exercise event Traci had organized. "I was not looking for anybody, especially with this new crazy body that I have," she said. But he pursued her, gently. "He had to overindulge when it came to compliments," she admitted. He would tell her she was beautiful, though she was too proud to tell him that she needed that kind of reassurance. "He just knew," she said. "I still felt, this is not my body, and I still didn't feel comfortable. It took us a really long time for us to even be intimate."

Before this relationship, despite all the efforts to enhance her outward appearance, she hadn't really looked at herself and how her body had changed post-surgeries. "I was so afraid. I would always wear something over my breasts, probably for a good six to eight months." Crucially for Traci, her boyfriend was patient. "You have to have someone who is extremely understanding," she said, knowing full well that some partners can't handle cancer and leave. It helped, she said, that he'd lost his grandmother to breast cancer.

Her boyfriend wasn't who finally made her comfortable in her body, though. It was a six-hour tattoo session. After her implants and surgery, one option was to have areolas reconstructed, but for Traci it didn't feel right to cover over the scar tissue. So, just before a weekend away with her boyfriend, she got a rose tattooed across her chest. "I am not a tattoo person at all," she said. "But it covers the entire top of my body. I was going to turn something that was, for me, something ugly, into something beautiful." That tattoo also declared, *My body is different now.* She was accepting it, letting it be more than what it once was. That helped her share it with someone else; she didn't need to hide.

Traci was able to do that, she said, because of her conversations with other women. They showed her that none of them liked how cancer was changing their bodies, but it was happening anyway. When she started being physical again, there was no hiding. Our scars and flaws are visible when we are intimate with someone else. Putting words to her scars and her journey through cancer helped Traci ease into sharing her body with someone else.

As Traci faced all this, first in her cancer support groups and then with her new partner, she was articulating something we all go through in different ways. Our bodies can become unfamiliar to us, through illness or aging, weight gain or loss, accidents or childbearing. Who we are, and the body we're in, can feel like they don't match up. Our bodies become a problem that we want to deny, cover up, and ignore. That snuffs out the kindling for intimacy, which requires exposing our physical selves, how they look and when they work differently.

Admitting that your body is changing, even when you have mixed feelings about it, loosens up some of that shame. What was once a secret problem that you tried to hide becomes a normal process you can talk about. Hot, dimly lit eroticism is just one kind of satisfying sex. After an open, vulnerable conversation about your changing bodies, connecting with someone in all your fleshy imperfections provides its own deep satisfaction and release.

Traci said that helped her embrace her body as it is, and made her feel grateful for what it still gives her. "I'm in a place now where I'm never going to have perfect breasts. I'm never going to have perfect thighs. But I'm still here."

———————

Talking about sex—whether it's with someone we barely know, or someone we've loved for decades—is hard. When we're starting a first conversation about sex with someone, we're often trying to maintain peak attractiveness. We want to be clear, yes, but we are also tracking where sparks are flying and in which directions. That doesn't leave a lot of room for awkwardness, sadness, confusion, shame, or fear of abandonment. But the fact is, all of us are needy, and our own kind of needy.

When sex and intimacy really feel good, there's room for some clumsiness on both sides, as psychologist Henry Dicks described in his influential 1967 clinical study of couples, *Marital Tensions*. He observed that "what makes 'mature' unions" is an uncalibrated and unsuspicious kind of love: a "childlike, unashamed dependence and its gratification by caressing words and actions."

Honest conversations about sex open the door to the needs we all harbor. And when it comes to sex, talking can also be playful—and very hot—if done with just the right whisper or cock of the head. Still, before it can be playful, it has to feel safe. That requires getting clear about what you both want out of it, as Ty Mitchell does, and disclosing the ways you need to be treated because of past hurts, as Karla has learned to do. Both are ways of naming the variables of shame, confusion, and fear. Conversation doesn't remove these as factors, of course, but it keeps them from just silently taking over the equation.

Because even clear, proactive communication about sex won't insulate us from hurt. Talking about sex and relationships can be heated and tense, just like any other difficult conversation. And, as in any negotiation, an agreement at the end isn't guaranteed. Accepting that rejection is a possibility is part of the deal, as Cord Jefferson learned. And talking directly about sex can uncover resentments and betrayals, as it did for Megan and Paul, or fears and hesitancies, like for me in my relationship with Arthur. These conflicts can be overcome, but it takes time to work them out together, and a willingness from both sides to delve into what *hasn't* been working and what each person will need to keep the relationship going.

Sex and relationships are exciting for the very reason that you don't know what will happen. An element of danger and mystery has always been present in our urge to connect. You might fail or be abandoned. You might have an unintended pregnancy, contract a disease, or fail to conceive the baby you've longed for. What you want could change fundamentally over time. And, as Traci Smith knows, your body itself will change, whether you like it or not.

Hard conversations don't get around any of those risks. But they can offer a bridge across the unknown, to find a partner who can navigate the dangers with us. Or, as Ellen Allen found, they can help you find the courage to set off anew: to name what you need—even in the face of judgment, hurt, and rejection—and ask for it anyway.

Money

I was in love and in a long-term partnership before I ever had to pay bills on my own. When I met the man I'd first marry, I was twenty-two and heading into my senior year at Stanford. Even though I was in the middle of Silicon Valley as Google was hiring its first big wave of employees, it didn't occur to me to try to get rich after college. Instead I was studying American history and writing a thesis on racism and civil rights protests in West Virginia. On a visit home to do research, I met my now-ex-husband, a funny, self-deprecating man slightly older than me, just out of law school, who was working at a small West Virginia firm specializing in civil rights cases. On our first date, he told me, "I'm a lawyer now, but I really want to make movies."

Oh yes, I thought. This really got me. I've always had a thing for creative types—writers, musicians, tattoo artists—but within reason. Before I'd met him, I'd started describing my type as "rock star with a day job." I was drawn to men who would bring adventure, excitement, and coolness into my life, but not introduce much risk.

He and I dated long-distance during the year I finished college. After graduation, I moved home, took a nonprofit job, and applied to law school, but landed my first journalism job and started working with public radio. We moved in together and started building a home, first with secondhand furniture, and then by shopping at IKEA, and then via the occasional splurge at the local midcentury vintage store. We shared bills and we shared a car. I would drop him off at the law office on my way to the radio station. When I was twenty-six and he was twenty-nine, we got married.

Then, after he turned thirty, my ex declared again that being an attorney for the rest of his life was not what he wanted. That intention he'd tossed off that had seduced me—that he was a lawyer but really wanted to make movies—was haunting him. "I want to apply to NYU film school," he told me about a year after we'd gotten married. "Okay," I knew to say first. Then I sheepishly added, "But what about me?"

He applied to NYU and got in. Then we learned he was awarded a fellowship that would cover his entire tuition. That can't-refuse offer made the decision for us: we would both quit our stable jobs with benefits and move to New York. I started calling around to friends of friends in New York about radio work in the city. But it was 2009, when journalism specifically, and the entire economy generally, was in free fall. "Don't come. There's no work," one audio engineer told me flatly. "Seriously, don't come."

But I was coming. I had to. This was my husband's dream, and it was coming true. In the months leading up to our move, I obsessively tracked our spending and socked money away. I thought watching our savings grow would help me relax about both of us quitting our jobs. It didn't. But I was embarrassed to tell him how scared I was about walking away from the life we'd had. And it wasn't like we could make a different choice. How do you turn down a full-tuition scholarship from NYU? How do you tell your husband, whom you love and want to support, that you don't want to go with him?

So we went, and I found radio work that mostly covered our expenses, including rent for a studio apartment in Brooklyn. We ended up only having to take out one student loan together during his first two years of school. The money part, the actual dollars in and dollars out, turned out fine.

But, in the process, our arguments about money revealed a much deeper problem.

———

Money is like oxygen. It surrounds us, flowing in and out of our lives—and when you're short of it, nothing else matters. Money is how we put food on the table, how we take care of people we love, and how we invest in all the things that express who we are. But money is also about so much more than what we buy. Money influences how we feel we stack up compared to others. It warps how we see our present and future, with either hope or dread. When it comes down to it, money often determines our very worth—in the deepest sense of the word.

"It is emotional and it's also this concrete thing," financial therapist Amanda Clayman told me on *Death, Sex & Money*. "It's two things at the same time. It's both a symbol and a tool." Amanda hosted a spinoff of *Death, Sex & Money* during the Covid-19 pandemic as unemployment numbers started to spike. The idea began when the team and I looked around for honest conversations about this dual nature of money and we couldn't find them. We wanted to hear people confront the reality of their money—what they had and how that was changing—and explore how those numbers fit into their values and sense of identity. *People need this*, we thought. At least I definitely do.

"It's a big taboo topic, and we're not used to having that conversation," Brad Klontz, a psychologist and certified financial planner, told me. He cofounded the Financial Psychology Institute in 2014, after he finished grad school with overwhelming debt and found himself alone with the mental burden of it. "I had no desire to become an expert in financial psychology. What I wanted to do was find the expertise already written and read it and then move on, but when I looked into the field of psychology, the topic of money had been totally ignored."

The first goal of this chapter, then, is to help us all be a little more honest about the emotional weight of money. Because, gauche as it may be, money is always there, forcing you to think about what it means to you (symbol) and how you choose to use it (tool). When we make financial decisions with someone else, or financial decisions that affect someone else, most of us are inexperienced at being direct. These are big, consequential conversations in intimate relationships—about what we value, how we feel safe, what our obligation is to others. It can take time and attention to root out the odd habits and meanings we've developed around money over the course of our lives. But without doing so, and without having the hard conversations that follow, we can't get into the gritty work of making intentional money choices with our loved ones.

In our most intimate relationships, though, at least we have the context that comes with direct knowledge of each other's spending and saving habits. When we move out of the private sphere of the household and into our circle of friendships and work colleagues, our sense of each other's money lives becomes more opaque. Even with people we're quite close to, everyone has an incentive to emphasize sameness more than difference. If you've ever had a friend inherit a sudden financial windfall or a family member run into dire financial straits, you've felt that slight chill of tension where there was once ease. But, I argue, the most honest and helpful conversations about money linger in those spaces of difference. They're how we see where we can help one another, and also help us understand how money is working in our lives with greater context.

We may think we're being polite by staying mum, but there are real costs to evading the reality of money for the sake of social comfort. Talking to colleagues about salary ranges and negotiations helps ensure you're not underpaid. Asking for help when you're in a crisis helps harness financial resources, and emotional resources, that you wouldn't know about alone. Sharing money stories also exposes the structural forces that enable some people to sail along and cause others to struggle, even while working identical jobs. Honest conversations about money can bring you more clarity, and more money.

The risk that stalls most money conversations is our fear of how we will look compared to the person we're talking to. We do a lot of sleight of hand to obscure how we're doing financially; this is true from our most intimate relationships to our national politics. We live in an era when tech billionaires wear jeans and sneakers, struggling people carry designer purses, and doctors and lawyers are drowning in student loan debt.

We avoid and evade because, even in a time of surging income inequality, no one wants to be an outlier in America. Most of us want to present ourselves as part of the honorable, hardworking middle class. "Despite evidence of rising income inequality in recent years," a Gallup report found in June 2017, "Americans are no more likely now than in the past to identify themselves at the high or low ends of the social class hierarchy." This is the way we have thought of ourselves, even as a 2015 Pew Center study found that the middle class is no longer the majority in America.

That's beginning to give way, pushed by protest movements like Occupy Wall Street and Black Lives Matter that have demonstrated how not every American has a fair and equal shot at success. In a 2020 NPR/Robert Wood Johnson Foundation poll, more people thought it was getting harder in the United States for an average person to earn a middle-class income, rather than getting easier or staying the same. This survey was conducted, NPR noted, just as the Census Bureau was reporting that income inequality in the United States had hit another record high.

Still, our deeply ingrained beliefs around money, and how we get it, are remarkably durable. In that same NPR poll, people across income levels were most likely to cite "hard work" as an essential driver of financial success. They also overwhelmingly said the American Dream is still attainable for their children and grandchildren. (Seventy percent of people earning less than $35,000 believed that, and the rates went up from there by income.)

We are confused about how we see ourselves collectively, so no wonder our interpersonal conversations about money can be so muddled! In our private lives, we do all sorts of verbal gymnastics to avoid the simple truth that, at any moment, how much money any of us has is the result of both our personal actions *and* many larger forces far beyond our control. Your financial situation depends on everything from the broader economy, to the year in which you were born, to the conditions for your parents and grandparents, to the whims of illness, injury, and chance.

When I'm interviewing people on *Death, Sex & Money* about their financial situations, I try to keep this in mind. I weigh how I'm emphasizing their personal choices against the systems they're a part of. If I ask too many questions about how someone decided to borrow money to attend an expensive school, for example, am I somehow letting policy makers and college administrators off the hook for shifting so much of the higher education burden onto students and their families? When it comes to money, our political debates tell us that we either condemn the systems and structures, or we condemn people's personal decisions.

This is a false choice. Each of us has acquired spending and saving habits, yes, but we are also helped or hurt by generational timing and the wealth or debt we happened to be born into. "Weath, not income, is the means to security in America," Nikole Hanna-Jones wrote in the *New York Times Magazine* as she made the case for reparations for Black Americans. "Wealth is not something people create solely by themselves; it is accumulated across generations." On top of that are the biases about whose work, time, and ideas are more valuable. Without being specific about the ways all these factors comingle, we chalk up big wins or shameful losses to our own personal characteristics. But that's not how money works.

The lasting goal of hard money conversations, then, is to identify which parts of our money worries are within our control and which aren't. We make personal money choices in the midst of larger systems: everything from the cost of housing to tax policy to social safety net priorities. Interrogating these systems is what drives our political movements and debates; and one-on-one conversations are not going to solve them. But by understanding where we are situated in these systems, we can shift some of the mental burden off our bank accounts. When you talk about the larger context of your own money situation, it becomes easier both to give and to get help. It's easier to ask for help because your particular challenges aren't just personal anymore, and it's easier to give help because you see how your good fortune is not just the result of your cleverness, so you ought to pay it forward.

The best conversations about money make room for both structural forces and our personal choices. They reveal the different histories that are part of our financial identities, along with the varied personalities and values we bring to our financial choices. When we can look at both aspects clearly, it becomes a lot easier to turn the conversation to practical dollars and cents.

It might seem byzantine that we often have to wade through so many layers just to talk more surely about the electricity bill. But that's why money is so tricky to talk about. And that's why rule number one is this: the best place to start any money conversation is to admit that money is about much more than money.

Which I've learned the hard way, because I have often been so bad at this.

"What do you want?"

I entered adulthood with a rigid set of ideas about money, specifically that there are good and bad ways to deal with it. For me, the good ways all minimized risk: getting and keeping a stable job, following the advice of professionals about how much you're supposed to save, and not spending money on anything that could be considered frivolous or flashy. (If you do buy something for yourself that you don't really need, I believed, it should be on sale.)

My clear prescription for being a responsible adult did not include quitting my job and moving to New York City in a recession so my first husband could become a film student. This contradiction lodged itself in my gut.

Saving money made me feel responsible, independent, and safe, and on the flip side, withdrawing money, any money, felt bad. And I was lucky that I didn't have a lot of practice with debt. I had no student loans thanks to my parents paying for college—my dad was a surgeon, my mom a physical therapist. When I was starting out in radio, my ex made more than I did at his law firm, but his father was not a surgeon—his mother was a teacher and his dad didn't work anymore. He had student loan payments and credit card debt from college and law school, but he worried about money less than I did. "You spend what you have," he would tell me when I'd get stressed about money after we first moved in together. "If there's a time we need to spend less, we'll spend less."

I found his breeziness comforting, because I was learning how to be an adult alongside him and was rattled by how much money life actually cost. I tried many things to snuff out my anxiety in the months before our move to New York—therapy, meditation, creative visualization—but the one thing that really worked for me was checking my bank accounts. There, I would see evidence of all my perseverating about money and security: regular savings, tightly controlled spending, retirement contributions. *You are responsible*, I would hear those numbers whisper back at me. *You are going to be okay.*

There is a term for my money personality type, financial psychologist Brad Klontz told me. It's classic money vigilance. I believe that money requires constant monitoring and alertness, and I feel responsible and like I'm doing the right thing when I obsess over it.

Vigilance is one of four money scripts Klontz has identified in his work. The others are money worship (money is the key to happiness), money avoidance (money is bad and corrupting), and money status (money ranks our value and deservedness). These represent the attitudes and values we carry into our discussion about money. We often realize their effect, like how they have shaped our choices about spending or saving, but not their source. When clashes of money personalities show up in relationships, they are explosive because they cut so deep. Money disagreements, Klontz told me, are "typically related to some survival impulse, which are the ones that are the most difficult to change."

Moving out of these ingrained money scripts requires unpacking where these beliefs came from and considering whether they are actually true. In the context of a relationship, examining each other's money habits can force couples to reflect and put words to responses that have become automatic, Klontz noted. It can encourage a curiosity about each other that "shifts the entire conversation away from hostility or anger or entrenched positions, because usually we're just trying to convince our partner that they're wrong and we're right."

In my first marriage, we never really figured out how to talk about the money scripts we each brought into the marriage, and which of those values we wanted to guide our lives together. Maybe, for example, I could have admitted I'm a scaredy-cat when it comes to calculated risks, so he and I could have batted around contingency plans until I'd neutralized my survival fears. Or we could have befriended a crotchety filmmaker type in New York, who could've buoyed my ex's dreams of a long career while helping me build faith that we could figure out how to pay for a creative life as we went.

We didn't do either of those things, though. My ex and I battled over every money choice: Was he going to take a summer job or use the time to work on scripts? How much of our money could he spend on this short film budget? Could we even afford this dinner out? How would we afford to stay in New York after he graduated from film school?

We didn't make it to graduation, though. Before that, the years of accumulated slights and resentments exploded when we were on a small plane, flying back to New York after a visit home to West Virginia. A clear plastic bag from Subway sat on my lap, with a sweating turkey sandwich inside. We'd been bickering and picking at each other all weekend. "I don't want what you want!" he finally yelled at me on the plane. "You want to have a house, a family, a regular job. I want film projects everywhere! I want to live in Europe! I don't want to be stuck!"

I stared down at my turkey sandwich. He was right. I wanted to have kids. I wanted roots and stability. And I didn't want to start over. But I didn't know what to say, other than to shush him, because everyone on the plane could hear. I was shaken to hear the fundamental conflict in our marriage finally articulated, and so clearly. The dynamics of our marriage had been upended by his career change to reveal that we had different comfort levels with financial risk. And maybe risk in general: he wanted a totally new life, and I wanted what we'd had. He felt hemmed in; I felt rejected.

There were other insults, as he retreated and I felt abandoned. I've debated whether I can sum up our divorce as irreconcilable differences about money.

That seems both accurate and too simple to capture all that had frayed. Neither of us was getting what we needed anymore. Where once we'd felt like a team moving through the uncertain world together, we'd become two separate and resentful people, pulling against each other and shredding what had once been a shared vision. To boil it down to just money felt too mundane for a loss that was so profound. This is what gets missed when conversations about money only focus on personal finance tactics, like joint accounts or splitting bills. What we wanted didn't match up anymore. We wanted to make different choices—with money, and with our lives.

Years later, I look back and feel tender toward my rigid, scared self who kept looking at her savings account for reassurance. And I marvel at my ex's courage to go straight toward an uncertain dream. His bravery made my life decidedly better. If we hadn't been married, I never would've moved to New York without a job lined up in the middle of a recession. And none of the rest of my life, which I'm quite pleased with, would have happened.

But our marriage didn't make it. About a year after we split up, I was on a road trip interviewing voters across America. At a café in Iowa, a farmer told me about all the booms and busts he and his wife had been through, and how many other marriages he'd seen collapse under the pressure. What made them different? I asked. "Well, to make it work," he said, "you've got to have the same plan." For my ex and me, all our money conversations about paying for life in New York were a distraction from a bigger misalignment. In the end, we didn't have the same plan.

Becoming single again at thirty, I learned that I could manage to take care of myself all on my own. When I was making all the decisions, spending started to come easier. Now it wasn't losing control, it was self-care! My hawkish vigilance seemed to calm down. It reappeared, though, as soon as I fell in love and had to share again.

"What is money for?"

My divorce, in retrospect, was like a braid slowly unraveling. How we did, and didn't, talk about money tugged and unknit us. We didn't have any major betrayals around money, just different objectives. That is not always the case.

A couple named Hien and Mitchell told me about a money quarrel that threw their relationship into turmoil, after one partner invested $100,000 of their joint savings in a vacation rental property and kept it a secret. It didn't end their relationship, but the two of them still disagree about how big a violation it was, because they have very different cultural beliefs around money.

"I knew I was helping out my family," said Hien, who had made the investment with his brother. "You know, I trust them." So, he figured, his partner should trust his family too.

Hien knew Mitchell tended to be more conservative with money, so he put off telling him about the investment. More than two years passed. And then Hien's brother asked for another $40,000, to cover renovation costs. It was more than Hien had in his joint account with Mitchell, but his brother was insistent.

"He said, 'What are we going to do, just leave this house? Then we're not going to make money out of it!'" Hien remembered. "I had to tell Mitchell. And I had to ask him, 'Can you pull some money out of your retirement account?'" When Mitchell found out, he was shocked and deeply hurt. He considered the investment a major betrayal.

Mitchell's and Hien's different assumptions and values around money had always been a source of misunderstandings between them, but they treated this as fodder for how they balanced each other out. When this major conflict happened, they had to figure out how to understand what had led to it.

Hien was a young child when he immigrated to the United States from Vietnam with his parents and four siblings. "Right at the beginning of the war, we'd lost everything," he said. "We went from middle class to extremely poor." They left Vietnam by boat in 1980, and as soon as Hien started public school in the United States, he was focused on achieving for the sake of his family. "I need to do well at school so I can get a good job, so I can help my parents out. That was really the big motivator for me." His parents were part of a cash club with other Vietnamese families, through which they pooled savings and loaned money among each other, so Hien learned early on that money management was all about relationships, ones often outside commercial banking systems. When his family arrived in the United States with so little, "Money did not define us. We were still a family," Hien said. "It wasn't attached to stability in the same way. We weren't afraid to start over again."

He and Mitchell now live in a duplex that they share with one of Hien's sisters, and Hien's sense of their intertwined fates with his family hasn't just been a source of pressure. It's also been a comfort—one, though, that's often been inscrutable to Mitchell. "He'll say, 'Don't worry. My family will take care of us,'" Mitchell told me. "I don't even know what that means!"

Mitchell is thirteen years older than Hien and grew up in the southern United States, in a community that he feels like he escaped. He's white, and when he was a kid his father sold cars and his mom ran a travel agency. "We were an upper-middle-class family," he said. "And then they lost everything."

Mitchell's mom struggled with alcoholism, and just after Mitchell left home to study music at an expensive private conservatory, she called to tell him she was losing her business. His parents, who had been paying for Mitchell's tuition and his apartment, were filing for bankruptcy, and he was on his own. Mitchell had to leave school and made money waiting tables. He eventually moved into a career in hospitality, married a woman, and then in his early forties, he came out as gay. When he and his wife divorced, Mitchell let his ex-wife keep most of what they had because he felt bad. So, twenty years after being on his own for the first time, he was starting out again financially. "I just constantly want to be getting rid of debt and setting aside money for savings," Mitchell explained.

Mitchell's sister, his only surviving relative, still lived in their hometown. She developed multiple sclerosis and struggled to get around outside of the home she shared with her boyfriend and two grandchildren she was raising. "She has led a very difficult life, and she and I have a somewhat strained relationship, but I try to help her financially." He said he spends two or three hundred dollars a month covering things like her electric bill or sending gift cards for the local grocery store, which feels more comfortable to him than just sending cash.

"I just try to help her as best I can," he said, and added that a lot of his giving is fueled by guilt. Unlike Hien, Mitchell's financial fortunes were something that separated him from his family and reinforced that he was on his own. "Somehow I got out and have a life that is relatively successful. There's always this question in my mind. *How did I do that? Why did I make it out?*"

When Mitchell and Hien met, they were both in the midst of resetting their lives and their finances. Mitchell was finalizing his divorce and Hien had finished college just a few years before. They both had work, so covering the bills wasn't a problem for them. They pooled their money together, and, like most couples, had some disagreements about priorities in their budget. Mitchell wanted to set up more security for them, in part because he is older and retirement feels closer for him. Hien likes to buy nice things with the money they've earned—the shopping app Gilt gets him good deals on luxury clothes—and he nudged Mitchell to enjoy how much they can afford to help his sister. "It's your family," Hien said. "That's what you do."

For years, this felt like the healthy push and pull of making decisions as a couple, especially because they had jobs that enabled them to save for retirement, buy the duplex to share with Hien's sister, and build up a sizable joint savings account. When Hien secretly withdrew money from that account, he told himself that he would tell Mitchell that he'd invested the money, that it was not only a way to do something to help his brother but also was a moneymaking opportunity for them. But then it became easier to just never bring it up. When he finally had to admit he'd secretly spent their money, he also had to tell Mitchell they needed to withdraw even *more* for the renovations or risk losing money that Mitchell hadn't known they'd spent.

"I just blurted it out. And it was hard. Like, he had no clue," Hien told me. Mitchell was devastated. "I felt quite betrayed and angry," he told me slowly. "It is something that has hung over us." Hien felt terrible for hurting Mitchell, but he also still felt like Mitchell didn't get it. "I didn't really, like, *apologize* apologize. I kept saying, but it's family. It's what we do with our family," he told me. "I said, I don't expect you to understand it but I wish you would just trust me. And he said, 'Trust you? How dare you bring that word up when you went behind my back.'"

They relayed this to me first in separate conversations and then again together on the phone, a year and a half after Hien had confessed. As they talked together about it, it was clear the betrayal had barely scabbed over. Mitchell told me that after Hien confessed, Mitchell then called their financial adviser to make sure Hien could no longer authorize withdrawals alone. They both needed to sign off, a move Mitchell felt stunned to have to make to protect their shared money. Plus, Mitchell would never have chosen to do this with their money. He already felt like they were spending more than they should and needed to be socking more away in their retirement accounts.

Hien, on the other hand, still trusts that they'll be okay, because he doesn't feel like it's all up to them. "My family will take us in and they would treat us like princes. I think that's the security that Mitchell doesn't have," Hien told me. "I think when two people get together and they're from such different backgrounds, you don't really actually talk about it until you come upon a conflict like this. It really forced us to say, *Wow, your background and the way you think about money is so different from the way I think about money, because of my relationship with my family*."

Hien remains resolute that his investment with his brother is the kind of thing you do for and with family. He knows he shouldn't have spent the money without telling Mitchell, but he doesn't regret it as a financial decision, in part because he doesn't view putting money in a vacation rental as less wise than a retirement account. It's simply another way to make money, and because he's doing it with his brother and not alone, he doesn't feel the need to be as cautious. Talking about this, at the time and then together with me, helped Hien and Mitchell see the starkly different ways they thought about being financially responsible. They had never answered the question together: What is money for?

That question teases out the threads that make up how we each think about resources, security, risk, and interdependence. The ways we learn about money, and these values, in our families and cultures are often not explicit. Until we articulate how we think about money, it's hard to make decisions with someone else, whose financial instincts may be quite different. Talking about these underlying values also gives you the opportunity to evaluate which beliefs you want to hold on to, and which you can try to let go.

For Hien, who has largely had a positive relationship with money in his family, money is for chipping in and to create more stability for himself and his extended family, even if they have done it in ways not usually prescribed by conventional American retirement consultants. Mitchell, who's been on his own and felt the tenuousness of relationships, just wants to follow the rules and protect himself and his partner. For one partner, money is for taking risks to benefit an extended family; for the other, money is for insulating himself and his partner from risk.

Mitchell got emotional as he listened to Hien on the phone. "Because I dearly love him. There are a lot of ways that I can't understand him," he explained. "But I feel like in a way this conversation has helped us to not tie a bow on it, but to revisit it in a way that makes me say, 'Okay, I understand it even more now,'" Mitchell told both of us.

"Oh really?" Hien chimed in. "So, you're not going to talk about it again? Good to know!"

They laughed, knowing this was not going to be the last time this comes up between them.

And moneywise, this all ended well for their investment. They sold the rental property in 2020, Hien told me. "We're getting that money back, plus profit."

"Shall we spreadsheet?"

After I filed for divorce, being back in total control of my money felt like a relief. I had learned though my divorce, like Hien and Mitchell did in their crisis, that joint money decisions are often about much bigger things than money. I didn't want to bother with all those lurking issues. I had a job, a stable lease on my apartment, and I knew that I was going to be okay financially. I was in control and I was going to keep myself safe.

When I met Arthur, he was making less than $30,000 a year as a grad student in Wyoming. He used what money he had and didn't think about it much. He kept his bills on autopay, and once in a while, if he really needed something he couldn't afford from his checking account, he tapped into funds he'd inherited from his grandmother—a small safety net he hoped would last until he landed a job.

While we dated long-distance, with him in Wyoming and me in New York, we kept our money separate, and when we were together we traded off covering expenses. When Arthur finally moved to New York, we started looking at two-bedroom apartments in Brooklyn so he could work from home. We found one that was just right—near the park for our dog and close to a grocery store and subways, but it rented for more than double what I paid for my first New York City studio four years earlier.

I was making more money than Arthur, even though he has two more degrees than I do. When we signed a lease together, we accounted for the disparity by opening a new joint account for shared expenses, with each of us contributing based on the ratio of our earnings. I paid more, since I earned more. This didn't bother me, actually. I didn't mind sharing, but where we differed was what we thought was an okay amount to spend on rent. For him, it was worth spending more money on a place that worked best for us. For me, when I thought about writing that big number on a check every month, my body tensed up and my breathing became shallow.

We ran the numbers over and over to show ourselves that we could handle the rent, and Arthur pulled up other listings to illustrate how this one was the best deal. Meanwhile, I kept telling myself, proudly, that my caution was the mark of responsibility. I was tapping the brakes to keep us safe from financial ruin, conveniently ignoring that this also allowed me to feel in control. Arthur pushed, I finally relented, we moved in, and we were fine. We could afford the place, and it was so comfortable that, a few months in, my earlier protests felt like a distant memory.

That didn't stop me from repeating this dynamic over and over again, including in the months after we got married in 2015. Arthur got a tenure-track job offer in California that we couldn't turn down. I had to ask WNYC to let me transfer out to California or face the prospect of losing my job. This activated my muscle memory from the move to New York years before. But this time, I was also pregnant. There were so many unknowns that I focused on what I did have a sense of: all the new expenses that were coming our way. From Arthur's point of view, my worry was taking the fun out of all the good things that were happening.

I interpreted this as evidence that he could not be trusted to be prudent.

This impasse led us to Patricia Kummel, a couples counselor and former attorney, who told us she focused on pragmatic problem-solving, which was what we wanted. We needed help agreeing on a budget for our move, our new life in California, and early parenthood. As Arthur and I listed off the number of life transitions we were in the midst of, she told us that outside of death or divorce, we had most of the big ones covered simultaneously: new marriage, new pregnancy, new job, new housing. Patricia asked questions that prompted us to describe our different money personalities, and after a few sessions Patricia gave us homework: to make individual budgets for our lives as parents in California. Then we could compare the different values we were bringing to the decision-making. I was sure I would win.

The next Sunday afternoon, Arthur and I sat in bed with parallel laptops and started building our spreadsheets. I made quick work of it at first. I was the one with all the bank and bill-pay logins at the ready, so as we set up the first rows of our budget, I called out relevant numbers like our average utility bills and grocery bills over the last twelve months. By this time, we'd stopped tracking earnings ratios and given up on separate accounts, mostly because it didn't feel worth the trouble after we married. Some people make different choices, but we decided that since whatever we borrowed or earned in our marriage was each other's in the eyes of New York family law, we could let go of that hassle.

Side by side, each of us filled in these numbers from our existing life on our separate spreadsheets. Then we set about estimating the costs of living in a place where we'd never lived with a new child. Arthur looked up things like parking rates on campus at his new job. I googled "how many diapers does a baby use in a day?"

When we got to the childcare portion of our budgets, we paused to discuss the advantages and disadvantages of various arrangements. We started envisioning how our new life as two working parents might look. We pulled up college savings calculators and talked about how much of our kid's college costs we would try to cover. Arthur calculated a monthly babysitting line item for date nights. Slowly, our discussion became less about money and more about how we wanted to use the money we had for this entirely new stage in our lives as a couple. I also noticed that Arthur was not entering spending estimates that were wildly higher than what I would have. They were based in reality, not in fear, and his focus on spending for our present—as opposed to my focus on saving for later—was another way of taking care of our family.

By the time we turned in our homework to Patricia, our separate spreadsheets had become one. We had our baby, we moved, and we began the long process of building a home for our family. Then we had another baby. We still fight about money, but we've updated that budget along the way to anticipate a few more years into the future. It can still be overwhelming and anxiety-inducing for me to look at. Between childcare and housing, our built-in costs are a lot right now. When Covid hit, I added a column to capture assorted "unknowns": possible media layoffs, university furloughs, childcare contingencies. These line items didn't fit into any spreadsheet calculation, but making a list somewhere to acknowledge how much could be in flux brought me a lot of reassurance.

I still have the part of me that gets panicky about spending—and I hear from her regularly!—but I can pull up the spreadsheet to show her that Arthur and I have taken her worries under advisement. That has cleared the way for my money conversations with Arthur to focus on the actual financial choices we're facing, instead of letting them become another contest between the feelings we have about money.

"I'm out of options."

When Arthur and I were noodling with our family budget, we were talking about our values and priorities, but we also had a lot of basic money questions that we asked each other. *Wait, how much do you think we'll owe in taxes? That online calculator says college will cost WHAT when our kid is eighteen? Do people really pay this much for housing in the Bay Area?*

Money management has always been confounding, but today a lot of us are increasingly isolated as we figure it out. Most of us don't walk into a neighborhood bank and sit down for a chat with a professional guide. Instead we go online, look up assorted personal finance articles, and manage our bills and savings with a few clicks every month while the number of bank branches is decreasing in America, closing at a rate of three per day over the last ten years, according to the FDIC.

If you don't have a romantic partner or a family member to talk to intimately about money, it can be hard to figure out who to go to when you're confused or overwhelmed. So you may put off dealing with it, until a financial emergency forces a conversation. "I spent a really long time not asking for help and that was not going well for me," writer Ashley C. Ford told me in an interview. "At what point do you just try something different and see how it goes?"

Ashley was raised in a family where it was normal to be direct about needing and giving money advice. She grew up in Fort Wayne, Indiana, with her mom working as a guard at the local sheriff's office while raising four kids, and her father was in prison. "Everybody always owed each other money," especially between her mom's four sisters and Ashley's grandmother. There was no shame in running short and asking for help, because the needs seemed to circulate constantly. "Everybody was always putting bills in somebody else's name or, can you help me get this car, can you cosign for me?" But that was all with one caveat: "You did not ask people outside the family for anything."

But when Ashley left for college eighty miles away at Ball State, she noticed a change. That network was gone, and in its place were credit card bills and student loan checks, addressed to her alone. Ashley paid for school with a combination of grants, scholarships, and loans that totaled nearly $80,000. Even with on-campus jobs, she couldn't always cover all her expenses.

A couple that Ashley calls her "college parents," Becky and Mitch, stepped in to help. They worked in student affairs at Ball State for years and Ashley babysat their kids. She could talk to them about money, but asking for help felt different from the conversations within her family. There was no getting around the power difference between them.

Then, when Ashley lost her housing at one point, Becky and Mitch invited her to stay in their basement. They also gave her money, which could have been really fraught, but Becky graciously and clearly laid out the terms. She told Ashley, "We don't give money unless it's a gift," Ashley told me. "I think what they were trying to say is, *We're helping to stress you out less. So if worrying about how you're going to pay it back is going to stress you out more, that's negating our intention. So don't worry about it.* I've been lucky to have people in my life like that, more than a few."

This challenged the way she thought about how people took care of each other. Growing up, she'd come to believe that "the best thing you could do for someone else is not need them," she told me. "To free them from the burden of you." That had made her resourceful and independent. But when Ashley did run into trouble, it meant she didn't speak up until she felt like she had no other options.

Ashley left college a semester short of graduating in 2012. "I couldn't afford to stay anymore." She had maxed out three credit cards and was working three jobs—two for different nonprofits and a copywriting gig on the side. She shared an apartment with two roommates. There was no give in her budget, but it worked for a while, until her car broke down and she had no money to fix it. She couldn't get to her nonprofit jobs on public transit and she was fired from both. "Then the copywriting dried up and they just stopped calling me," she said. "I had nothing. I had nothing except a place to live."

Since she didn't have rent money, she told her roommates that she couldn't afford her share of their $1,100 monthly rent. She intended the conversation as a heads-up that they'd be missing her rent payment, but they surprised her. "They were just like, we got you," she said. They didn't make a formal agreement or set a schedule for her to pay them back. Instead, her roommates treated it like a temporary emergency. "They were pretty much like, *We like you living here, and we love you. Stay here. We don't want to go anywhere. If this becomes the thing we can't handle, we'll let you know,*" Ashley remembered. "*Otherwise, chill. Look for a job.*"

Hearing this simple, loving assurance—that she was not alone in this crisis and it wasn't a big deal that she needed some help—shifted her out of her panic and gave Ashley the space she needed to be deliberate about finding both her next job and work that would be meaningful for her long-term.

Her roommates covered her rent for two months. Ashley got work at a call center, made $600 by selling her car to a junker, picked up some freelance writing on the side, and paid her roommates back in about four months. Within the year, Buzzfeed recruited her as a writer and paid her way to New York. She arrived there with $800.

Ashley picked the right people to talk to when she felt like she was out of options. Without their help, temporary financial emergencies could have easily compounded into a life-altering, years-long spiral of debt and missed opportunities. When it comes to financial advice, or actual monetary assistance, what works in one relationship will not necessarily work for all close relationships. "Not any economic transaction is compatible with any intimate relation," Princeton sociologist Viviana A. Zelizer has written. She calls herself a "relational economic sociologist." In other words, she's an expert in the art of figuring out who is the best person to ask for help when you need it.

In both instances when Ashley ran into a financial emergency, she had to summon the nerve to admit she didn't know what to do. Before she knew how to ask, someone else offered to step in with financial help. These were delicate conversations, because Ashley's dignity was on the line. "I resisted their help a lot," she said. As she let them step in, she discovered a profound new kind of love existed outside of family. "I was not their responsibility," she said. "These people were teaching me there was more for me in the world than I thought there was."

How these conversations unfolded told Ashley as much about the kind of relationships she had and could have with these people as they did about money. Or, to put it more academically, "People work hard to find economic arrangements that both confirm their sense of what the relationship is about and sustain it," Zelizer wrote in a paper with the grabby title "Do Markets Poison Intimacy?"

Markets, and money, do not have to poison intimacy, but they can complicate it. Borrowing and lending money can create a concrete grudge to point to when something else goes awry in your relationship. When you're in a tight money spot and need help, choosing whom to talk to about it is as important as what you actually say.

Ashley eventually finished her last college credits and is now comfortable financially. With a bustling career of writing, speaking, and podcasting, she gets asked to give money to people she loves. She uses the same techniques that made her feel comfortable when she was the one asking. Her mother does not ask easily, but when she does, Ashley assures her that she is freely giving what she can, and it's not going to lead to resentment. "I handle it by saying, 'Mom, I promise I will never make myself broke to help you.'" She said that while she considers herself generous by nature, "I try not to be reckless with my resources. I may be broke one day, but it won't be because I gave all my money away. Not even to my mother." When she's had to say no to some requests for money, she is direct and clear. "A nice 'No' or 'I can't right now' shouldn't mean losing someone you love, and if it does, is that love?" she said. "Quick answer: no."

She learned another critical lesson when she allowed herself to need help. Living through her own money emergencies, and being able to help others through theirs, has reinforced to Ashley that money crises and uncertainty can be temporary. They are not a verdict on our inherent worth or deservedness. Adding the qualification that this is a problem *right now*, as opposed to describing a problem as an endless state, focuses the conversation on the current problem-solving. Once Ashley assesses the need and urgency of the request, she makes a simple calculation based on what's she got available—without getting bogged down in moral judgments about who deserves what.

"I know how hard I had to work to make nothing," she added. "I know how hard my mom had to work to make practically nothing. Knowing how I live now, and how much money I make now, and what I have to do to make the amount of money I make now, it's, like, it's still work, but it's absolutely nothing like what my mother or my aunts or my grandmother had to do to make a living.

"It's not close as far as how hard it is on the mind and the body," Ashley said. "It's not close."

"We're coming at this from different places."

In moments of crisis, people in Ashley C. Ford's life showed up to help, with both advice and money when she needed it. Some of the support came from older mentors, where there was already the built-in dynamic of guide and student, but she also got help from her roommates—her peers—who pitched in without making her feel like a pariah.

But sometimes differences in access to money and wealth create real and lasting shifts in how we orient ourselves in close relationships—like those with coworkers, friends, and siblings.

Naming these differences is important, even though that can feel antithetical to closeness. Otherwise, unspoken differences can become silent resentments. So as you're getting to know a new friend, include your backstory about how your parents did financially, and how that helped or hurt you. Your money history is a main driver in who you are and where you've ended up. Swapping these stories also makes plain how the economy is working differently in each of your lives. Talking about this helps both of you see that your relative fortunes are partially the result of larger, structural forces. Awkwardness, guilt, and envy will be present whether or not you say there's a money difference between you. You might as well confront it.

I talked to author Cynthia D'Aprix Sweeney about this, because she got famous for writing about money in detail in her bestselling novel *The Nest*. Published in 2016, her novel centers on four siblings angling around each other as they await an expected inheritance ("the nest"). Unlike her characters, Cynthia did not grow up with a lot of money. "There is no family money in my family, quite the opposite," she said, laughing. "My parents are generous to a fault, and I always joke that I'm just hoping they don't leave behind debt. That would be really good."

She didn't really understand the impact of inherited wealth when she arrived in New York City after college. "I didn't actually believe that trust funds were a real thing that real people had," she said. She would notice her coworkers, who had the same job as her, buying new clothes she couldn't afford and taking vacations she could only dream of. "I'd think, *Am I just terrible at managing money?*" Because the reality of how money worked in her peers' lives was unspoken, Cynthia just assumed she wasn't measuring up because *she* was doing something wrong.

As she approached thirty, she became hell-bent on figuring out how other people were making it. "I really became obsessed with how people managed to afford to live in New York City and have a family, which is something I very much wanted to do," she told me. "I would sort of poke around and the answer was always family money. It made me hateful, in a way that I felt terrible about."

Hateful, yes, but no less dogged in the pursuit of uncovering her friends' personal financial histories. Becoming a mother helped the information-gathering. "Having kids gives you an in to other people's lives in a way that just being friends doesn't." Cynthia remembered meeting a mom in a neighborhood pizza joint in Manhattan, "and then, sort of mom-flirting and making eye contact, we started talking and I really liked her." Her new friend invited her over, Cynthia remembered, "and I stepped in one of the most beautiful apartments in New York I've ever been in." It was enormous, with large windows framing views of the Hudson River. "And I just looked at her and said, 'Oh my God, how much was this apartment?'" Cynthia remembered. "And I was so immediately mortified. She turned beet red and started talking about what a good negotiator her husband was, so I didn't really get an answer."

Cynthia had assumed sameness when they'd hit it off, when in fact there was a lot of difference. That made the clear contrasts in how they lived seem extra mysterious, the result of a simple life hack that Cynthia had somehow missed. "I think I really felt like, *There is a secret tunnel! That's how you get an apartment*," she said, laughing. She knows now not to blurt out that sort of thing, and now, of course, she could just go home and look up that apartment on Zillow. She later found out the husband, the good negotiator, was also a banker.

Having their differences acknowledged out loud is what made that conversation so awkward, because, again, we've all been trained to tamp down our varied financial positions, especially among peers. Cynthia's husband was no banker. At the time, he was an aspiring stand-up comedian and comedy writer. And as awkward as that exchange was, it really helped Cynthia not to get down on herself when her life didn't look like some of her friends'. She slowly became more confident in opening up conversations about why that was. "It became a little easier to say things like, 'I would love to find a place we could afford down here, but I don't know if we can do it,'" Cynthia told me. "And sometimes people would say, 'Well, you know, we wouldn't have been able to do it either. My dad gave us the down payment for the apartment,' or 'I inherited some money from my grandmother.' And it did feel like it was coming from a compassionate place," she said. "Like, *Don't feel like we figured something else out. We didn't. We just got lucky in this way.*"

Learning this didn't make Cynthia feel less envious or the world seem more fair, but at least she didn't feel like a chump who had messed up. Her struggles with New York real estate weren't her personal failure. Once you got down to it, in many cases the difference was access to family wealth. This wasn't comfortable for Cynthia to accept, but at least she finally understood.

Then Cynthia's financial position changed. Her husband got a regular writing gig on a new show, hosted by a young comedian named Conan O'Brien, and at first it just felt like a godsend to have a regular paycheck every month. "We were just, like, if we could pay off the Visa bill, that would be amazing." They ended up saving $30,000. It was the mid-1990s and they were able to buy an apartment in Brooklyn with 10 percent down, after ignoring the advice of everyone who told them it was unwise to buy without 20 percent. Five years later, they sold that apartment for $700,000—more than double what they'd paid for it—and they bought a brownstone.

They made money on that house too when they sold it to move to Los Angeles and bought another nice house. So nice, in fact, that after Cynthia finished her MFA in creative writing when she was in her fifties, she felt embarrassed to invite her classmates over for a graduation party, especially knowing how many of them were struggling to cover their bills. She didn't know exactly how to address this difference either. She wasn't used to thinking of herself as the one in the more comfortable financial position.

Big transitions in financial standing often come with complicated feelings. "It helps explain why lottery winners blow all their money," financial psychologist Brad Klontz told me, when we talked about the social anxiety that can come with moving up. "Because it creates such anxiety to be outside of their financial comfort zone, outside of their family and friends, that they get rid of it and then it's like they're not stressed anymore."

Klontz calls these comfort zones "socioeconomic tribes," because losing or gaining money can separate us from our community and threaten our sense of belonging. "For people that are in your same financial comfort zone, it's much easier and safer for you to talk about how much money you have invested, how much your income is for the year," Klontz explained. "It's a lot less risky."

Cynthia felt that unease and tried to downplay her success, even though it was clear from where she lived that her class situation had changed dramatically. Then Cynthia sold her debut novel, *The Nest*. "I sold the book for over a million dollars and it was a news story," she told me flatly. The book was based on writing she'd done in those graduate workshops, and she could no longer hide how much she was moving ahead financially from people she considered her peers, because it was all public knowledge. "I remember saying to my husband, 'I'm never getting out from under this narrative,'" she said. "But honestly those questions went away once the book was doing well. No one asked about the advance anymore."

Her money situation changed before her sense of identity did. She still thought of herself as that hustling kid who showed up in New York City without connections, who came from a family without a financial safety net. "My three younger siblings, like most people, are trying to make ends meet. They have good years and tougher years," she said. "It's hard to have more than the people in your family." Cynthia explained this to me slowly, carefully. She knew she sounded like a complaining rich white woman, and she knows how it stings when someone close to you is doing well when you're having a hard time. "I feel like I used to do this with my friends who I felt, you know, had things that I wished I had. I'm sure I said a lot of really sort of subtly diggy, underminey, inappropriate things like, *Well, it'd be nice, I wish we could stay in this neighborhood, I wish we had that kind of money*," she said. "I wasn't trying to make someone feel bad, but maybe kind of in a way I was."

Now that she's on the other side of this economic divide, what she used to have in common with her siblings is something they don't share anymore. She's learned that, for her, the best way to deal with the weight of those tensions is to just admit they're there, with care not to belabor the point. She's generous with her money, and when she shares, she keeps the conversation short, to acknowledge the gift but not in a way that overemphasizes it or could make her siblings feel embarrassed. Like when she got a royalty check from *The Nest* around the holidays one year, she divided it up among her siblings' families and their parents: $2,500 for every member of each family unit, plus some extra for her parents. Along with each check, she wrote the same note, explaining that it was an unexpected windfall and that she wanted to share it with them. "I said thank you for being nothing like the characters in my book," she told me. "It was fun and it was nice. I also realized it's not going to fix that I wish we were all in the same exact situation."

A conversation was never going to erase the differences in their financial positions, but acknowledging that difference helped Cynthia eventually get used to it. "It's a little self-indulgent to make yourself feel bad in that way for a long time," she said. She kept jumping in when she felt like she needed to, like when her parents had high medical bills. These transactions didn't come with long, drawn-out conversations with her family. Instead, she'd quickly note that she was in a position to take care of an expense, so she would. It all stopped feeling so fraught.

Then she started doing this publicly, and gave up the urge to downplay her success. In August of 2020, Cynthia announced that her and her husband's family foundation was going to invest $100,000 to fund a new fellowship program in publishing for graduates of historically Black institutions. She'd just finished another novel and gotten a payment that was years in the making, her kids were out of college, and she'd had some conversations with an adviser about how to manage their charitable giving in a way that was more organized. That adviser told her to think about what she cared about. She was in a position to give money to make the field of publishing more accessible, but still, she initially wanted to make the contribution anonymously.

"I was uncomfortable," she said. "I was worried it would come off as self-aggrandizing." But her publisher, who helped set up the program, talked her into using her name, convincing her that it was significant that an author who had done well was now contributing money to create opportunities for people who didn't always know how to access the insular world of publishing.

Uncomfortable as it was, Cynthia decided to make her contribution public, to bring attention to the fact that there are, in fact, secret tunnels. Not to fancy city apartments that are affordable for everyone, like she'd wished for as a young mom, but to a wide array of opportunities. When you don't have money, or the resources that come with proximity to money, it can be hard to even know where to start.

"This is a systems issue."

Financial emergencies can be sneaky. When we don't have enough to pay for what we need, deciphering between a temporary setback or a life-changing comeuppance can, at first, feel like a matter of attitude. Credit cards or short-term loans can cover a shortfall, and that debt can seem opaque and abstract, so you're left to spin it as you see fit. Is this a signal of a wrong turn, or a test of your resourcefulness?

"The trouble with denial is that when the truth comes, you aren't ready," Nina LaCour wrote in her novel *We Are Okay*. Danielle Muñoz sees a lot of unready people in her office. She runs the crisis assistance center for students at Sacramento State

University, where enrollment hit record numbers as the rate of local rent increases topped national lists. Her job is designed to help students in any kind of crisis, but since she started in 2016, it's money that brings students to her door. "You'd think it'd be all over the place, but it's not. It's all rent-related."

Danielle told me that when she first meets a student, she starts by offering what she calls "precision care." Before talking about numbers or choices or the housing crisis in California, she thanks students for just coming in. "I really recognize that it's really hard for people to ask for help, so hard that I think people go years without asking."

Students usually come to her after revealing to someone else on campus that they're in a financial emergency. "Most students don't come forward and say, 'Hi, I'm not housed.' They'll say, 'I'm not going to be able to do the work you assigned me because I'm going through this.' That's where the stigma is," she said, so a lot of her work is making sure instructors and faculty know where and how to refer students to her.

That was exactly the case for a student named Alejandra. She was referred to Danielle by an instructor who'd noticed she was visibly flustered after she turned in a test. Before Alejandra could rush out, her professor stopped to ask if she was okay. "And I just started crying," Alejandra told me. "I told her that I was probably not even going to finish the semester because I had to get a job and help my husband."

Alejandra was in her mid-forties and had been working toward her degree for more than six years, first at a junior college part-time, and then full-time to try to finally finish her degrees in child development and Deaf Studies. When she'd started at Sacramento State, her husband's job at an insurance company was enough to support her and their three kids. "We knew it was going to be a sacrifice, but we didn't account for him being out of work."

Then, he was laid off, she told me, "and then he got another job, and then he gets laid off a year after. Then he goes a year without a job, and then he gets another one and gets laid off. It's been like that on and off." When we first talked in 2018, Alejandra's husband was working as computer repairman on contract. "Right now, if he lost his job, I don't know what would happen," she told me then.

As she tried to finish school, she cobbled together grants and student loans to cover tuition and her family's costs. "Then it ran out," she told me. She couldn't make the math work, particularly in Sacramento, where Alejandra had lived for twenty years but the cost of living was becoming steadily less affordable. Her family paid $1,400 a month to rent their three-bedroom place "and it's not even a nice neighborhood," she said. "We don't have good credit because of consequences of unemployment and everything else, so you get what you get."

And as Alejandra sat in class that day, trying to finish a Child Development 136 exam, she knew her family didn't have the money to cover tuition for that semester. At her instructor's urging, Alejandra went to Danielle's office and explained how her family's long, once-manageable slide had become a housing emergency.

Danielle listened, then pointed out the broader structural issues. "I do offer a little validating, like, this is not a character flaw. This is a systems issue," she explained. But Danielle has to balance acknowledging those big forces with creating an action plan. *"It's nothing you've done wrong, you didn't cause it, but here we are having to solve it,"* Danielle told me she says to students. "It takes a level of radical acceptance."

When Danielle spoke the words "radical acceptance" to me, I first thought it was a California way to talk about what most other people would just call acceptance. But Danielle explained that radical acceptance is a form of cognitive behavioral therapy developed in the early 1990s. "It's about managing your emotions, and facing the reality of things," Danielle summed up. "Hardships are unavoidable. So, if we know that, we can get to the action part quicker and we can start doing something with it." When it comes to money, that means confronting the larger economic forces as they are, as opposed to wishing they were different.

The *radical* part of radical acceptance is key, because it's not just acceptance. Danielle is not telling students to just concede or surrender. Instead, it's learning to say, *Even if I don't like this, or I think it is unjust, I have to deal with this reality*. For example, Danielle told me she personally reaches out to landlords to try to negotiate discounted rents, goes to local council meetings to advocate for more affordable housing, and personally wrote a grant to develop a rapid-rehousing program so her office could offer emergency shelter for students who were losing their housing. When she's talking to students who are in a financial crisis, her focus is not only to empathize with their difficulties and lament the system together, but to steer the conversation to available resources and an individual course of action. That's radical acceptance.

Danielle sees her role as equipping students to navigate education goals and their budgets with as much information as possible. She goes over various resources and options, reviews the students' budgets, and explains aid disbursement timelines. If a student asks Danielle to solve the problem for them, she will say, *"I'm not a fixer. I'm a helper.* Because they are an adult, and I want them to be able to take credit for their success." She will also commiserate with them that their current available options, like moving into a place with roommates, might not be what they had pictured for themselves, but she stresses that they are not permanently stuck. They are doing what's necessary to finish their degrees, and these compromises will have an expiration date.

For Alejandra, she and Danielle went over Alejandra's family budget and what she would need to graduate. Part of the plan they came up with was taking on even more debt, and Alejandra remembered a lot of discussion about what that would mean, making sure she understood when the scheduled payments would begin and how much they would be. She also applied for a grant, funded by Sacramento State donors, for students in financial emergencies. "I had to write a paper explaining how this was going to help me stay in school," Alejandra said, which meant looking directly at her family's financial reality.

Like with Ashley, Alejandra told me her financial emergency clarified whom she can talk to about money, and whom she can't. Most of Alejandra's husband's extended family live nearby, but they are competitive about money and material items. Alejandra told me her sister-in-law once looked her up and down at a quinceañera and asked where she got her vintage dress and how much she'd paid for her shoes. "We Mexicans are supposed to be a big old family and support each other, but that's not the case in this situation!" she said with a laugh.

Alejandra appreciated having a neutral expert to talk to about her finances. In those conversations she could focus on her story and the numbers without having to simultaneously manage a relationship or an unspoken subtext about whether she was asking for money. But to get that help, Alejandra had to admit to herself that she needed it, that the tears in that classroom were a breaking point. If she had kept quiet and slunk away, she would have ended up with a lot of student debt and no diploma.

Alejandra finished her degree with $85,000 in student debt in 2018, when the average debt load for graduates of four-year colleges and universities was around $29,000. After she finished, she got a job she loves at a local preschool, one where the school requires teachers to have a bachelor's degree. She is paid $15 an hour and doesn't have health insurance. It's not enough, she said. "My field of work is underpaid," she told me. "You're not going to make a lot of money. It is what it is." This is *another* systems issue.

For some, Alejandra's debt load for her degree makes no financial sense. But when I asked her if school was worth it, Alejandra did not hesitate. "Yes," she said. "It's a lot of money with interest and everything, but I have my diploma that I can look at for the rest of my life." And, at least in the first years out of school, she didn't have to make payments, between income-based deferments and payment suspensions because of Covid-19.

She told me that other things worry her much more than her student debt, like her kids. Her oldest graduated from high school during Covid and her plans for starting community college were dashed by the virus. "It was a huge disappointment for her." Alejandra remembered that same feeling of helplessness, when big, uncontrollable events threatened to undo all she'd worked for.

Alejandra knew there was nothing she could say to her daughter to resolve the situation. But Alejandra recalled the sense of relief that she'd felt when she finally walked into Danielle's office. "Before that, dealing with all these issues for years, I would never talk about it, until I was crashing," she said.

Now she knows how to be there with her daughter, to listen and to guide as they distinguish between the factors they can control and those they can't.

"Who's getting wealthy? Why are they getting wealthy? What are they doing with the money?"

The way work is rewarded with money in this country does not reflect the worth of the work or the labor that's gone into it. For preschool teachers, the national median salary in the United States is just over $30,000. I host a podcast and make more money than my husband, who spent seven years getting graduate degrees and usually puts in more hours a week teaching, advising, fundraising, and writing.

"There's this weird thing that happens where we talk about money and its tie to work," Facebook cofounder Chris Hughes told me in an interview. "Most Americans are working. It's just that only a select few are getting very, very lucky." He is one of those very, very lucky people. He was Mark Zuckerberg's college roommate at Harvard and is a cofounder of Facebook. When he was twenty-five, Chris got his first bank statement that showed a million dollars to his name. "That would have been 2008," he said. At the time, he was working for the Obama campaign, making $65,000 year. It was still four years before Facebook went public, but he could sell some of his shares on a secondary market. "Most early employees did that as a way of taking out a kind of insurance," he told me. "I sold a million dollars' worth of stock then and no one around me had any idea."

He said this to me in the fall of 2017 when I interviewed him onstage at the San Francisco Mint at an event hosted by the Economic Security Project, a group that Chris co-chairs that advocates for a guaranteed income for all Americans. The program billed our chat as "A Frank Conversation about Money." And it was, though he demurred when I asked his current net worth. "For three years of work at Facebook," he did tell me, "I made about a half a billion dollars." The audience in front of us gasped and laughed nervously. Chris continued, "Meanwhile, median wages are stagnated and normal working people can't make ends meet. And I think these things are related."

Chris is the only child of a paper salesman and a teacher, and he told me that he still goes to his parents for advice about money. "It sounds crazy, because they never had an experience like this. But their relationship to money is so healthy," he said. Chris and his parents can't connect on the dollar amounts, but they have similar values about how they should manage what they have. "I still do all the things that they do. They tithed every single Sunday, and I do a lot more than that, but that kind of rigorous budgeting and accounting is something that I look to them for."

That said, Chris did admit that in his daily life now, he is very frequently the richest person in any room he walks into, and he also doesn't have much exposure to people making less than, say, $50,000 a year. "It's really hard to get out of a bubble and to have disarming conversations that are honest," he told me. Still, he tries, and for all his money, he doesn't feel like he belongs in the tech gazillionaire scene. "I feel more like an interloper in the sense that, like, I have very much become part of the inside, but I still really relish challenging the conventional wisdom that poor people, working people, middle-class people don't know best," Chris said. "I find that that's the status quo in a lot of the conversations that I'm in."

In other words, in rooms full of people with money, they're all pretty confident that they've figured out something essential that poor people simply haven't. As Pew reported in 2017, compared to lower-income people, people with higher family incomes are more likely to believe a person is rich because they've worked hard, as opposed to any advantages in their circumstances.

Chris has tried to pierce that mythology of meritocracy by talking about how he became so wealthy, which is how he came to discuss his personal budgeting style in front of an audience with me. He said it's not always comfortable, but it had gotten easier as he challenged himself to be more personally open. "I've learned that it's just money, you know?" he said to me. "There's a responsibility that comes with it, but you can talk about it in a way that recognizes its power and also helps people make collective decisions about how to move it."

Minutes after our public conversation ended and we walked offstage, I found Chris alone in a corner of the greenroom, nervously looking over the trays of snacks. He told me he wished he hadn't tossed off the line "It's just money" at the end of our conversation. He knows the risk of being seen as a clueless rich-guy donor, or, worse, a careless steward of immense wealth.

I assured him I got his point—that he was trying to articulate that money is a tool, but one that doesn't confer worthiness on people. That didn't seem to comfort him. I asked him if he wanted to elaborate on what it had felt like to talk so candidly and publicly about his money. When we connected again a few months later, he acknowledged a particular kind of loneliness. He felt compelled politically to detail what his personal story revealed about inequality, but being open about his wealth also highlighted a social distance he wished he could shrink. "With money, it can separate you from other people, and it's something that you don't want to be boxed into." He knows it's easier to just glide past that, but he believes that he has an obligation to sacrifice his social comfort for something bigger. "I think, on wealth, we haven't really broken through on the taboo," Chris told me, "of talking about how the economy works, who's getting wealthy, why they're getting wealthy, and what they're doing with the money. We assume those who have it have worked hard for it, fair and square."

We all know that's not the whole story. So, if you have more money than you need, talk about how that happened. We're used to acknowledging the big rewards that came from risk or hard work, but don't skip over your lucky breaks and inherited advantages. You'll be telling a more honest story, and one that may make you feel less alienated from other people, because you don't have to pretend that you are more worthy of comfort and reward than others to justify your wealth.

The social strain of wealth may not be something a lot of people without wealth have much sympathy for, but that doesn't mean the strain is not real. A wealthy software developer named Vik described this to me on *Death, Sex & Money* in 2018, for a series we did about class in America. "You know, in fairy tales it's a little easy because when Cinderella gets ahead, [she's] surrounded by mean stepsisters and a mom and an environment that wasn't helping and it was unfair," Vik said, continuing:

So when you arrive upon some really awesome destination, you're supposed to sort of go, "Well, they deserve it, and the other people were mean." And I think the reality is that, at least in my case, you find yourself here but along the way there weren't mean people. In fact, it's *because* of all the people that were around you that you got here. And not everybody's at the same place. And so you're left wondering about that.

When you take opportunities to acknowledge when you're doing well financially, you can talk about success in a way that also indicates what's important to you. Do you feel grateful because you have enough to help out your extended family? Have you created job opportunities for others? Has it allowed you to contribute to causes you support? As you acknowledge all this, you are also drawing boundaries around what you want to spend your money on, and what you don't.

That's what Chris tries to do. He describes how he came to have this enormous windfall, and now Chris straddles the work of developing particular policy prescriptions to change how the economy works and paying for that advocacy as a big donor. He's faced plenty of skepticism about whether he's an appropriate spokesperson. "He is an unusually self-aware multimillionaire philanthropist. But he still is, and behaves like, a multimillionaire philanthropist," read a *Vox* profile of him in 2020. When you're the richest person in the room, you wield power that others do not. That power is there whether or not Chris admits it. Still, I'd rather have more wealthy people publicly grappling with the ways their personal experiences match up with stories we tell about opportunity and success in America.

Chris is a critic of the jackpot he landed on, and yet feels like he can also take some responsibility for it. He didn't just win the lottery; he worked on the early team that invented a new platform that changed the world, for better or worse. As he wrote in his 2018 book *Fair Shot: Rethinking Inequality and How We Earn*, his story demonstrates that the current risk-and-reward calculus is wildly out of balance: "In a winner-take-all world, a small group of people get outsized returns as a result of early actions they take. These small differences that later yield big successes are often called luck, but luck isn't really the right word." A lot of hard work was involved to get into Harvard, and then to get Facebook off the ground. "But the combination of those small events led to outsized and historically unprecedented returns thanks to the magnifying power of today's economic forces," he wrote. The current economic system is designed to reward people in just his position, and it is a system, he argues, that is subject to change. "We are its authors and enablers."

Chris had become a father in the months between our two conversations. I asked him if that had changed his intentions for his wealth, which he had told me he and his husband planned to give away. "I want to make sure our children have financial stability in their lives and have every opportunity that I can afford them to find what they want to do and to pursue their dream, and that takes money." But exactly how much money and when this months-old infant could expect it were things he needed a little more time to work out.

"I don't really have a view that the best thing is to pass down from generation to generation just for the sake of it. And specifically, in my case, I made a lot of money for a modest amount of time working. It feels like I have a responsibility to give that away to things that make the world a better place and that leaves it a little bit more just," he said. "I've got this. Let's make it useful."

Our comfort with talking about money is deeply tied to what we think our own financial situation says about each of us. When you simply don't have the money that you need, it can usher in a sense of fatalism about what we can each control—not to mention the panic of trying to make ends meet. If you have a sense that most of your money comes from your own labor, it's easier to take pride and feel honor in your station in life. When your financial comfort comes from the work of others, sometimes those who lived long before you, you can doubt your deservingness and struggle to find peace with your story.

These narratives about money, and its meaning in our lives, are both ubiquitous and unconscious until we have to make money decisions with someone else. Our most intimate relationships expose our values around cooperation and independence, stability and risk. These conversations are the bridge between how we grew up imagining our lives and what type of life is attainable for our adult selves.

In close relationships, it's often easier for these conversations to focus on concrete numbers—a budget or a credit card statement. Sometimes that's all it takes. But when we skip over the values and principles that underpin our individual money scripts, as I did in my first marriage, it can cause hard money conversations to miss the mark and leave important power dynamics around money unspoken.

If your conversations about money are hitting a wall with your loved ones, it's worth backing up and exploring your assumptions about how money works. Money is tied up in personal history, family history, and culture, as Hien and Mitchell found out. Once you can discuss that, you can go back to the numbers and the spreadsheet, as my husband Arthur and I did, to use money talks as a way to fortify a shared plan.

Between friends and colleagues, money conversations make visible the differences that, for reasons of social lubrication, a lot of us were taught to downplay. Yet when we actually discuss money directly, these conversations can have underrated benefits, from closer friendships to smarter spending. Ashley C. Ford learned just how empowering conversations about money can be when she talked with mentors and friends, and in doing so, she created a support network for herself and others. At the same time, conversations inside friendships about the brass tacks of dollar amounts are essential for learning about how to manage our finances.

I've been so helped by generous mentors and peers who've described how they've asked for raises, when they turned down jobs, and how much they paid for childcare. These conversations are important, but they're also delicate. They are private and rely on trust. While some argue for greater transparency all around, I'm personally not comfortable shouting my salary from the rooftops, because to me, that strips the numbers of their context, which is important. I will readily share the story of my earnings history with a friend or close colleague over a drink: what I made when, how another job offer helped me negotiate, when I turned down an offer because it just wasn't enough. The difference there is that I'm having this conversation within a relationship, where we're able to talk about the stories that accompany the numbers.

So I'm not arguing for zero privacy when it comes to our money. To feel safe, we have to let each other make individual decisions about how and when to share. This information is personal, and as in conversations about sex, each of us may have different boundaries about what's okay to disclose. What I'm advocating for is a broader acknowledgment that money is an important factor in all of our lives, no matter how much we have. Keeping quiet about something so central sacrifices opportunities for more honesty, more closeness, and more interdependence.

Still, these conversations can be awkward and stir up negative feelings. As Cynthia D'Aprix Sweeney found, talking about money often means noting differences in who makes more or who got lucky. These differences are important to say out loud, though. We don't all start out in the same place; we don't all have the same chances. When we don't talk about money with the people in our lives, we are also less equipped to be honest and clear about how we want to handle the money we have and see clearly how money is shaping our society. At Sacramento State, Danielle Muñoz and Alejandra talked directly about the financial realities of living in an unaffordable housing market, and that recognition has helped drive them as they try to make their community more economically humane. On the other end of the spectrum, Chris Hughes realized that even what some would call a "self-made" fortune isn't so simple, which is why he speaks up to critique our belief in meritocracy and the balance of risks and rewards in our current economy.

Too often, we opt out of conversations about money. We make financial decisions without being intentional about the values that steer them. We privately worry about how we measure up next to the people around us. We tell simple stories that align money with effort and personal worth, when the larger, more consequential forces behind what we each have are far more tangled. Talking openly about money won't flatten differences between us, and it won't alone make money operate more fairly.

But these hard conversations do make money less mysterious. They give us some essential company while we go through highs and lows, and they help us separate our money anxiety and guilt from the actual dollars and cents. That is, they can lift an enormous weight—and make us more clear-eyed about what we have, why we have it, what we might do with it, and how we could work together for more.

Family

Within an hour of agreeing to end my marriage with my ex, I called my parents to tell them.

They'd known I was having a hard time, not from what I'd confided to them, but more from the tight, clipped way I'd assured them for months that everything was *fine*. When they picked up the phone, I don't remember speaking words, just the mix of sobs and exhalations that communicated, *My marriage is over*.

It was night, so late they must have been in bed, and I remember exactly what they said back. Hearing these words felt like falling into a giant cushion.

"Let me get your dad on the phone too," my mom said, and then cooed as I kept crying. "We are here, we are here."

"We're here. You have a good family," my father chimed in. "And I know just how you feel."

He did know. More than thirty years before, he'd tried to grind his way into saving *his* first marriage. He knew the shock of not being able to hold a family together even when you'd told yourself over and over that family was the most important thing. He knew about trying so hard and coming up against the limits of your control.

"You're exhausted and you can't sleep," he said to me, "I know, I know." Hearing this recognition from my dad, when I was still minutes into this failure, was so loving. My marriage was ending, and I wasn't alone. That phone call reminded me that parts of myself were still familiar when so much else was abruptly shifting to past tense.

That's what family can be at its best: a loving slot to fit into, where we are known and protected from the outside world. But family can also be painful—full of fights that don't make sense and wounds that never heal. Often we find ourselves bouncing somewhere between the two, from joy to frustration, from distance to reunion. This isn't unusual by any means. Family, after all, is where we learn how to fight, and come to know that loving and liking someone don't always happen at the same time.

For me, this was a lot easier to accept as a child, when battles in the backseat of a station wagon were routine. You want to cross the line and get too much in my space? I'll scream or bite your arm! That doesn't work so much as an adult. I'm a proudly independent middle child in a family of five daughters, one who deeply loves my parents, but I never particularly loved being parented. Figuring out how to feel close to my family in adulthood, while also enforcing adequate space around me, has always been a very hard thing to talk about.

When I mention family in this chapter, I see it both as the subject of many hard conversations, and a setting for them. We need to talk about family *within* our families. By and large, I'm talking about our families of origin—our parents and grandparents, our siblings and stepsiblings, our children and nieces and nephews. These are the people who teach us about belonging, identity, and responsibility. They show us who we are and where we come from. But they inevitably fail us over the years, in ways small or large. For some of us, our families of origin show us we'd be better off building an alternative network of loved ones.

Trying to talk about family conflict is uniquely hard—whether you find yourself navigating an unexpected flare-up or a long-considered rift, or more likely some combination of both. Our family relationships are the longest of our lives, and paradoxically they're often the most resistant to change. First of all, breaking up the usual pitter-patter of your family's routine is, on its face, a disruption. Many hard conversations need to break through years of studied avoidance. And dredging up old history then presents an opportunity—which most of us will take!—to relitigate guilt and blame, who said what, and which bridges were burned.

"Family is where we tend to lose our maturity," Michael Nichols, a family therapist who's written several academic and commercial books about family therapy and relationships, told me when I interviewed him. We may aspire to be patient, loving, and kind with the people we're related to, he told me, but we're often reactive, indignant, and closed off. "Most of us become teenagers in the presence of family members." That's because who we are in our families is built on long-standing patterns and roles. We didn't get to know these people as evolved and charming adults; they know our triggers, and often created them.

Hard conversations within families are so difficult because of that intimacy, and how that closeness shifts over time. We know our family members' insecurities and instincts better than we know our own. These people are so familiar to us, and us to them. But in reality, they know a version of us—who we once were—that can feel outdated or stifling as we grow up. Hard family conversations, then, have two critical purposes that can feel at odds. We at once want to understand our origins and connections to these people. But we also want to declare how we are different from them, and for our individuality to be understood, respected, and appreciated.

When I interviewed comedian Hasan Minhaj on *Death, Sex & Money*, he remembered a question his father taught him when thinking about how to approach conflict: "Do you want to be right, or do you want to be together?" Do you want to listen and resolve the conflict, or to stand firm in your convictions and your truth?

We want both, of course. But figuring out which we want more, at any given moment, can be our guide to when and how to approach uncomfortable conversations within families. Sometimes you do need to be "right," and declare that you are the authority on your life. To be heard and listened to, even if it contradicts how the other person thinks and feels, is the bedrock of mutual respect. In families, there can be abuse, bullying, and patterns of behavior that you can't talk people out of—no matter how hard you try. Drawing a line about what you'll tolerate is sometimes the only thing you can do.

Other times, it's more important to feel the connection that family can provide, to come together, even if that means letting some disagreements go or old conflicts release without resolution. And many conversations will dance between these two poles—independence and connection—depending on which you find more pressing in the moment.

We should expect to feel this tension between togetherness and autonomy, especially as we grow up. When the poet and filmmaker Rafael Casal was on the show, he talked about how he had dropped out of school to pursue hip-hop and poetry. His parents did not approve, and family life grew tense. "We were really just trying not to be angry, because they didn't understand a lot of my choices," he explained. "We were still navigating our distance."

I love that turn of phrase: *navigating our distance*. It's specific about the problem—feeling pulled apart from the people who were once closest—but it doesn't assign blame. Rather, it makes feeling distant where there was once closeness sound perfectly normal, which it is. After all, becoming an adult, by definition, means separating from the family members we grew up with.

I will never forget when I was a very new mom, constantly attached to my new daughter, physically and emotionally. Every grunt or utterance prompted an examination of its cause. I was talking to a parent with older kids, and she said to me, a little mournfully, "This is the closest you will ever be. Parenting is all about letting go." While it may be natural, letting go and separating from our family members doesn't always feel good. Because we long for family to feel like home. But a sense of belonging and closeness that was once intuitive can fray. The people who were once your sole guides to the world can disappoint you and run out of answers. Even in families where there's not major conflict, there are still rifts that emerge as we grow up.

When that happens, either because of conflict or judgment or because it never *was* true in a particular relationship, part of the pain is the simple fact that family doesn't feel like what our idea of family should be.

Family can also be the site of even deeper wounds and betrayals. Some families are places of abuse, abandonment, and mistrust, which can affect our relationships for the rest of our lives. Not everyone in a family is capable of being part of a hard conversation. Some family members lie and manipulate and degrade us. Others retreat and avoid stressful scenarios that often arise within families, preferring to keep things light and contained. Hard conversations within families may expose the limits of what you can expect from them.

Done well, hard conversations within families make room for the various perspectives each of you bring, while still acknowledging the connective tissue between all of you. That's what I want this chapter to help with. I want to describe the terrain of family so you can better see the ways in which some family conflicts and strain are inevitable parts of growing up—from childhood into adulthood, or from parenthood into old age. I also want to help you judge for yourself when there needs to be more direct conversation within your family. Conversations between family members don't necessarily make strains disappear. Instead, they allow each of you to explain yourself and how you understand your history together, as well as to describe how you are changing. Sometimes these are conversations where you need to deeply listen. Other times it's more important to speak up. Sometimes you need to feel right, and sometimes you need to feel together.

To decide which one is more important, though, sometimes you have to stop talking for a while.

"Let's talk. I listen and you talk."

Inside our families, our roles get cast early on. And with those roles come a set of unspoken rules about how you are viewed within the family, how you will treat one another, and who is allowed to say what.

Psychologist Murray Bowen developed his theory of "family systems" in the 1950s and 1960s, though he noted in later writing that it "contains no ideas that have not been part of the human experience for centuries." He designed a practice to help people recognize the roles they play together in a family and shed the patterns that aren't working. During Bowen's therapy sessions with family members, he asked that only one person speak at a time, and that they talk directly to him and not to one another. The hope was that as they took turns speaking in front of one another, the family could hear each other anew. He wanted to stimulate separation within families, or "differentiation," as Bowen called it, with the goal that each person could learn to be "an individual while in emotional contact."

By trying to listen to one another in a totally new way, you make room for family relationships to evolve out of their familiar ruts and grooves. You don't have to be *only* who you've always been to one another. In families, when we're all adults, more separation may create space for more love.

I talked about this with Yesi Ortiz, a host for a pop radio station in Los Angeles who raised her six nieces and nephews on her own. Yesi's sister struggled with substance abuse, and when her six kids ended up in the foster care system, Yesi petitioned for sole custody when she was just twenty-five. That meant she had to testify against her sister. "I had to say, she's not fit right now," Yesi told me when I first interviewed her on *Death, Sex & Money* in 2015. "I had to tell the truth." Yesi and her sister have not had a relationship since Yesi testified in family court to get her sister's parental rights removed. She told me she has no regrets about that.

When the kids first moved in with her, the youngest was five and the oldest was twelve, and Yesi organized her life around caring for them. Back then, she worked the early-morning shift at a radio station, so she'd leave the kids home with a babysitter when she went to work at four a.m. She picked the kids up from school, and would oversee homework, naps, dinnertime, bedtime, and then do it all over again. While raising them with her job was lonely, it was also proof that with enough will, she could do something no one else thought was possible—raise and provide for six children on her own.

When I spoke to Yesi again for this book in 2019, her youngest son had just turned eighteen, and now that all the kids she raised were adults, she was reflecting on her years of mothering them, and what kind of relationship to expect from them now. She became their mother when she got legal custody of them; now they legally no longer needed a parent. The years leading up to this moment had been difficult. As the older kids each became adults, they pulled away from Yesi in different ways. It had been hardest with her oldest son, A.

Around the time he turned twenty-one, A. had been getting into car accidents, wasn't contributing financially to the household, "was just being reckless," Yesi reflected. Her worry for him turned to exhaustion and she felt backed into a corner. "I couldn't tolerate his irresponsibility, couldn't tolerate his lack of respect anymore in our home," she said. "I told him, 'If you're not going to help pay the bills or go to school like you're supposed to, then there's no reason for me to provide a roof over your head.'"

Yesi was disappointed and angry. After so many years of pushing and worrying about her kids, she had little patience for A. entering adulthood without a drive like hers. "I was trying so hard to be a good parent, and no matter how I tried, I still failed," is how she remembers feeling at the time. "I always thought they'd know how much work I was putting into providing, or how tired I was after fifteen- or sixteen-hour days. I expected a lot from him, knowing the opportunities he had. He didn't take those opportunities for himself. I think that really disappointed me."

Since she'd gotten custody, Yesi worked hard to create a place of refuge and stability for her kids. How they handled themselves as young adults felt like an important verdict on how well she'd parented them. She also worried about the example A. was setting for his younger brothers and sisters. When she told him he had to go, he went to live with his biological mom, which felt like an additional betrayal to Yesi. "That's when I started realizing that they're always going to have a connection to their biological mom. As hurtful and painful as that was for me, I had to accept that," she said. "I can't control any of them and dictate who they can and can't see."

Realizing she had to accept the limits of her control was one thing, but learning how to communicate differently as a result was another. Yesi mourned the distance she felt from A., and initially she tried to mend it by asking him about his plans for the future. She wanted to make sure he understood the responsibilities of adulthood, but he didn't want to engage. That made her more frustrated with him and more uncertain about herself as a parent, still with five children at home. She'd seen up close how her sister's choices as a teenager had spiraled out of control, in ways that hurt her and many others. She didn't want that for any of her children. So just like Yesi did when she got custody of them, she wanted to continue to protect all her kids by taking control.

"To give them space was scary," Yesi admitted, but she didn't have a choice. The more she tried to police her oldest son, the less he wanted to talk to her at all. Over the next four years, as her other kids also became adults, the tensions with her oldest son eased a bit. He moved into an apartment with his girlfriend, they had a child that they are raising together, and he worked steadily at a fast-food restaurant and a convenience store. "I want more out of life for him," she told me. "We don't argue. We just don't see eye to eye on things sometimes." She still occasionally peppers him with questions about what his plans are and how he's going to make them happen. "Now he sits there and listens. He's not walking away like a big kid now."

She's had to accept that her role with him right now is being the person who's going to push him. When he doesn't want to hear that, he's going to talk to someone else. A. never told her this directly; he just withdrew. "Looking back, I definitely could have been like, *Let's talk. I listen and you talk.* I didn't do enough listening," she reflected. "I was so busy telling them how they should live their lives that I didn't listen to how they wanted to live their lives."

Yesi finally understood by talking to her next kid, her oldest daughter, who joked directly with her about needing to rebel to have some room from Yesi and make a few questionable decisions. "She literally said to me, 'I'm not going to tell you because in my head I already know what you're going to say: you expect more from me,'" Yesi recalled. "And she laughed and said, 'But I'm still going to do it anyway!'" Her daughter told her that making her own decisions is part of growing up, so back off. Yesi heard her, which also helped her see her oldest son's choices as *his* choices, not a reflection on how well she'd imparted her ideas on how to live.

This revelation shaped the way she talked to A. and how she felt about their entire relationship. "I don't put so much pressure on myself. And since I don't put so much pressure on myself, I can have more uncomfortable conversations," she told me. "I just simply say, 'Hey, I don't have the right words to say, but I want you to remember to always take care of yourself.'"

Letting go of her authority over her kids has let her be a little more honest about her own uncertainty. Yesi has a lot less control than when she was enforcing bedtimes and homework assignments, but in talking less, she's trying to reserve room to get to know her children better, especially as adults.

"Each child is different. Listen to what they're saying. Hear them," she reminds herself now. "They're going to come back around. They know I'm here."

"Here's who's helping me."

What happens if you're in A.'s position? What if you're the family member who needs some distance from the set patterns, expectations, and control of the rest of your family? How do you make that space?

An option that most of us have tried at some point is marching into our bedroom and slamming the door behind us. That makes the point. But in adulthood, it can be much more confusing. Especially if the need for space isn't because of some kind of explosive conflict, but instead an accumulated sense of distance that slowly stacks up as our lives diverge.

That's what a man who asked to go by Adrian described to me. Growing up in California, his life was tightly organized around his sprawling Filipino American extended family. They were a constant presence in his life, and he felt very close to his family, especially to his mother. But as he got older, married a white woman, and struggled with depression after his wife had two miscarriages, he noticed a rising sense of resentment that, for the first time, he felt like his family didn't know how to love him in the way he needed.

When Adrian was growing up, he always felt an easy belonging within his family. He was born a year after his parents arrived in the United States, where they moved to join his mother's siblings. "My mom had eight siblings and they were all trying to move to America. So they were helping each other out," he explained. "I remember there was a summer when there were four families, fifteen to twenty people, in a two-bedroom house." But instead of being annoyed by the tight quarters with so much family around, it made things fun for Adrian. "There was so much joy and laughter growing up," he said. "In my family, they always say, 'Family comes first.'"

Adrian went to a local college and graduate school, and big family gatherings continued to be a constant in his life. Every Catholic holiday or life milestone came with a crowd of aunties, uncles, and little cousins, including at his wedding to an Irish-Catholic woman from the other side of town, the side with money.

His wife got pregnant with their first child soon after they returned from their honeymoon in Paris, just as they'd hoped. But at their first doctor's appointment, there was no heartbeat. Her body didn't know her pregnancy wasn't viable, though. "She was still having the worst morning sickness, so to have all the symptoms but to know what you're carrying is not alive . . ." Adrian trailed off. "For about a month, she was essentially carrying our dead child, which was very hard for both of us to think about at the time." Even after two rounds of medication, her body still didn't expel the dead tissue, so she went in for an outpatient extraction. She nearly hemorrhaged during the procedure, the result of an abnormality in her uterus that doctors hadn't known about, and she had to be hospitalized.

This was just their first miscarriage. A few months later, they got another positive pregnancy test, and within a few weeks, bleeding signaled that this pregnancy was also over. Adrian and his wife were devastated, and for Adrian, being around his big Catholic family didn't provide him any comfort. "The way that they deal with grief is to give it up to God and to pray and to do rosaries and things like that." His family's casual mentions of God's plan, or the comfort of going to church, were infuriating, because Adrian was so angry with God. "Those miscarriages changed my spiritual life, completely changed my relationship with God," he said. "I always thought there was some kind of justice if you tried to do things right and you try to live your life the right way. That's kind of a stupid thing to think, actually. I was pissed."

Regular family gatherings became awkward and uncomfortable. "We forced ourselves to go," he said. "They were all trying to be very delicate, to talk about things with me that they would never talk about. Cousins who hate sports would ask about the [Sacramento] Kings game," he told me. "It made it so much worse, you know. There were all these well-meaning people who kept checking in, in the wrong way." He's not sure, though, what the right way for them to check in would have been. He just missed that easy feeling of togetherness he'd had before. Nothing at that point in his life felt light or easy, so when his relatives tried to connect, it felt like painful playacting. Looking back, he sees and appreciates how they tried, even though he wasn't ready to accept their efforts to comfort him.

Adrian and his wife had a daughter in 2017, a year after their second miscarriage, and their first years as parents continued to be challenging. His daughter had health problems and his wife struggled with postpartum depression, while Adrian worked full-time and tried to hold it all together. The distance he felt from his family was like a constant drone in the background, something he couldn't turn off. "I was such a big part of my family, everything that we did, and I'm not now," he said.

But his mother kept trying to show up in ways that would support her son. She watched her granddaughter at Adrian's house four days a week while he and his wife worked. He was grateful, but still couldn't shake the feeling of lost closeness.

Finding his way back took time. The disconnection from his family was based on real differences that hadn't always been there. He felt disillusioned with Catholicism after the miscarriage. He was married to a white woman and had earned a master's degree, a level of education most of his extended family didn't have. And it was also his sadness, which didn't fit in with his family either. "My mom's mantra growing up was there's not enough time in your life to be sad. Just get on with it," Adrian said. "That didn't work this time. So I went to a therapist, which is not something my family does."

But he felt like he needed to confess to his mom that he was getting counseling, and why he'd been feeling so apart from her and their family. "I told her I was having a really, really rough time and I needed some outside help." Adrian was afraid she would react with judgment or try to talk him out of feeling sad. To his surprise, it prompted her to start a broader conversation about how their lives were diverging, something they hadn't admitted out loud. She'd known he was struggling, and was glad to hear he was getting help—even if it was help she herself didn't know how to offer.

"She told me that she understood that moving to America necessarily meant that her kids were going to have a different experience," he said. Their family was loud and loving and joyful, she admitted, but also rigid. "She told me that she was proud of the man I'd become, proud that I'd been strong for my wife, strong for my daughter," he said. "And she said if I were to differ from my family in some kind of way, she knows I can handle it." Hearing his mom say that ended up helping more than the therapy did.

Telling his mom about his therapist gave Adrian a way to acknowledge that he was having a hard time, and also to relieve the pressure on her and his family to help solve it. And Adrian could admit, without guilt for the first time, that his family couldn't, and didn't need to, provide all the support he needed. "That was really helpful because I felt very different from my family in a lot of ways," he said. "[My mother] understands that even though I'm not following the family's path, it's still a way to be successful. That was important for me to hear."

"I'm drawing a line."

We are entwined, often over many decades, in the lives of our family members. Conflicts and tensions come and go, and we have to decide what is enough of an issue to need a conversation, or when we should quietly note our disappointment and try to make it okay. We have the gift of time in ways we don't in other hard conversations. These relationships, and conversations, unfold over years and decades within families, with ebbs and flows in closeness and understanding.

"Honestly, with families, you do, in a lot of ways, close your eyes to the things that bother you. You have to give everyone the benefit of the doubt," filmmaker Desiree Akhavan told me. "Because you're married for life."

We put off conversations to keep harmony and compartmentalize as needed. But sooner or later, some unavoidable fact can get in the way of a wish to keep things copacetic, like decline and aging, necessary money negotiations, or stark value differences when it comes to how you want to live your lives. "If your moral compass is different from your family, there's nothing that can replace living on your own terms," Desiree explained. "Being honest with your family is really valuable, but it is also very uncomfortable. But it's worth that discomfort."

For her, falling in love with a woman in her mid-twenties forced her to disappoint her parents, without apology, and it changed everything. "I didn't realize how much lying and trying to please others were dictating my own happiness. I don't think my life started until I put my foot down," she revealed. "You draw your own line."

Desiree was born in 1984, just a few years after her parents and older brother immigrated to New York from Iran. From a young age she was aware of how much her parents had given up for her and her brother to succeed. "We were very aware of sacrifices that had been made," she told me. Her family viewed themselves as outsiders in a new land, but because Desiree was the only one of her family born in the United States, she was also the one member of her family who was more apart from the rest of them. Her older brother has "always been a bit of a third parent," she said. "He and I had different approaches to being in this family. He had a lot more responsibility and felt like he was the anchor in the house. Because I was the younger one, I got to disappoint them."

Growing up, she felt like she had more room to break convention in her family, which played a role in making her feel like she could tell her family about her girlfriend. "I knew I had to tell them, and I told them, and it was really bad," she remembered. She was visiting her parents for the weekend, and on Sunday evening, she told them she needed to talk. "I said, I have to tell you something and you're not going to like it," Desiree said. "My dad just didn't talk. I could tell he was broken. I totally broke him." This was devastating for her. Both her parents had trouble accepting her because it was not what they pictured for their family. "It had a lot to do with image. I mean, I think my parents saw some sense of, *We're going to have to carry this like a scarlet letter*."

Desiree's parents needed time to metabolize this new information. Not only did they fear she was going to live "a second-class life," Desiree said, they also didn't understand. "There is a level of self-indulgent self-exploration that comes with being American. They thought, *Why wouldn't you keep your private life private?*"

She couldn't say anything to make their discomfort go away. For Desiree, this process helped her learn to listen to the little voice telling her when something is off, the voice that can cheer you on when you draw hard lines. "I think that's how you end up creating boundaries, through having that kind of voice." Boundaries took some effort to fashion in a family where, in an argument, her father routinely throws down the line, "You forget, I created you," Desiree said. "That's the argument: *I created you*." She said this with affection, but was also clear that when he says it, he's not kidding.

But she knew she needed to tell them. "The alternative was to lie and I wasn't going to do that." In cases where that clarity isn't there, figuring out when to speak up about something that will unsettle your family is difficult. When do you decide to create that conflict when everyone knows their place in the status quo? "The timing is never right," Desiree bluntly observed. If you're waiting for the window when you'll know just what to say and how to contain your family members' reactions, it will never happen. "It's about living in the discomfort and putting out there something that you know someone doesn't want to hear, because if you don't, it festers and it becomes a huge explosion and it's harder to contain."

In her family it took years, but her parents have settled into the reality of who Desiree is. "They made a really big switch." Desiree later asked her father what finally changed. He told her, "I had one of two choices: lose my child, or get over it."

It also helped, Desiree joked to me, that she quickly achieved success making semiautobiographical films about her sex life. "The taboo became the shining star."

Family can be many things, positive and negative, but most of all, it is familiar. New revelations disrupt these familiar patterns, but they also create space for outdated dynamics to reset. "Coming out opened up the possibility of messiness," Desiree said. "We were freed of this unspoken expectation we'd placed on ourselves of representing the ideal immigrant family."

About five years after Desiree came out, her parents divorced. Their marriage had long been tumultuous, going back to when Desiree was a kid. Her parents treated their fighting as normal, but to Desiree it didn't feel right, or safe. "I would always call them 'episodes' when I was a kid. It was like you were in a movie, the severity of it. You didn't know what home you were coming home to," she told me. Back then, she spoke up in her family and at school about it, but nothing changed. "Everyone was like, 'Desiree, you're such a drama queen.'"

When her parents' marriage was over, that story also abruptly changed. "Everyone was like, 'You were right.'" That has kicked off a whole new series of changes in her family, shifting what they expect and ask of one another now that they're all adults. "It was so natural when we were kids and we had very tangible needs. We all just want to understand each other a little bit better and understand how to be each other's family."

But, as Desiree learned, these shifts don't happen if no one speaks up.

"I understand." (Sometimes, say it even when you don't.)

When someone speaks up in a family, the person starting the hard conversation is not always the one in the family who is best suited to take the lead in a tough conversation. Power dynamics get fixed early, between parents and children and siblings. It's often the person with less built-in power who has to figure out how to adjust the script.

A woman who asked to go by Anne learned this early on, when she realized that, while her mother was in charge in their household, she wasn't always a reliable narrator. Anne's mother has what doctors now call schizoaffective disorder, a combination of depressive and manic symptoms along with psychotic hallucinations and delusions. Anne is in her mid-thirties now, but when she was growing up, neither she nor her mother had words for what was happening. "It was a lot of unexpected chaos, not knowing how she would be one moment to the next."

Anne was eight when her mother was hospitalized for the first time. "I remember coming downstairs and seeing everybody in the family room very concerned, sitting and talking around my mom, and overhearing that she had checked out of the hospital and walked several miles home." A few years after that first hospitalization, her parents divorced. Her two older sisters left for college when Anne was thirteen, so managing her mother's illness fell largely to Anne.

Anne quickly learned that her mom's triggers included lack of sleep and stress, so she'd do whatever she could to avoid upsetting her mom. "I got trained as a young person to please other people because it was a survival technique that I had at home with her," Anne told me. "I knew it would keep her calm and make her happy if I did well in school, or if I didn't talk back. I appeased her in whatever ways that I knew would make her feel good."

Still, the paranoid episodes came. Anne's mother would become convinced their house was tapped by the FBI, or decide she was in danger in the middle of the night and barricade herself in her bedroom. And then there were the times her illness spilled out of the privacy of their family. Once, Anne's mother picked up the phone while Anne was talking to her best friend and "started spouting off some paranoid stuff like, 'Who is in the house? Who is in the house?'" Anne recalls. "I had to hang up real quick." A few days later, "mortified and embarrassed," Anne went over to her friend's house and tried to explain. "I told her, 'My mom is not always with it,' and I remember feeling surprised and relieved by the compassion she showed me," she said. "I had felt like it was a reflection on me in some way."

Anne left home for college and became a school librarian, which she attributes to having to seek out answers quietly on her own while growing up. (She says she first started looking for words to describe her mom's behavior on AOL with dial-up internet.) But Anne still lives within an hour of her mom to help her manage her psychiatric care. Her mom has been hospitalized several times since Anne's been an adult, including in May 2016, when Anne was on vacation in Oregon with her boyfriend. She got a phone call from the local police department near her mom's house, with the report that her mother was causing disturbances: yelling across the courtyard, slamming doors and banging things in her house at night, and harassing neighbors she thought were a threat. This had happened before—that's why Anne had given the police her cell number.

She flew home from vacation early to help manage the situation, and as she boarded the plane, she desperately googled for any new answers. She found an e-book called *I Am Not Sick, I Don't Need Help!*, a guide for caregivers trying to convince someone to accept mental health treatment. Denying there is a problem is a symptom of many psychiatric disorders, psychiatrist and author Xavier Amador wrote, one that made managing his own brother's schizophrenia more difficult. "My natural instinct to confront denial of illness head-on led to disaster," he wrote. In its place, Amador offered the acronym LEAP: listen, empathize, agree, and partner.

This acronym, and its spirit of collaboration with willful dishonesty and pretending, were not how Anne's conversations usually went with her mother. When her mother was in crisis, Anne would desperately try to pull her back into reality-based thinking, pointing out how what she was feeling was not real: no one was after her, she was safe, and what she was assuming was wrong. "I'd always tried to talk her into sanity and convince her that her thinking wasn't clear. I would just fight, fight to be heard, fight for my mom to acknowledge what I was saying," she said. But trying to talk her mom out of her delusions "was always beating my head against the wall. It never got me anywhere and just caused more pain."

This book encouraged Anne to accept her mother's delusions in their conversations, to ask questions about them, and, crucially, to agree with her mom so they could partner on her care. "Even though it's not fully honest, it still felt like the most dignified way to treat her, and to treat myself," she said. Anne's new approach in conversations didn't fix her mom's condition, but by the end of this week-long hospitalization, the way they interacted for decades had started to shift. "It wasn't a magic wand but I believe it brought us closer."

When another crisis hit a year later, Anne tried LEAP again, and this time the stakes were even higher: the neighbors were complaining again, and threatening to use the condo association rules to force her mother out. This was just the kind of thing that would make her mother feel under attack, fitting into the logic of her delusions. Her mother had been convinced that someone was spying on her and trying to poison her, so Anne focused on that sense of danger with her mom, instead of trying to talk her out of it. She found herself saying things like, "Gosh, that sounds really scary. It sounds like you're really worried people are breaking into the house." She observed after, "I don't have to agree with her delusions to validate her feelings about them."

This time they didn't fight about which threats were real and which weren't. Anne knew she was playing along with her mom's faulty premises, but that's exactly what allowed them to move the conversation beyond that moment toward what needed to happen so her mother could stay safely in her home. "I felt myself behaving in my adult capacity, more calm and less like I was thrashing and out of control," she told me. "It helped bring her guard down. My mom felt like I cared about her well-being and I was there to help her."

This time, her mother agreed to go to the hospital and stayed for six weeks, her longest hospitalization ever. "She was more vulnerable, a little softer," Anne said. She started taking an injectable antipsychotic medication, and before she was discharged, her mother signed a document authorizing Anne to make mental health care decisions for her in the future. "I remember sitting with her and holding her hand and having conversations that we had never really had before, communicating in ways that we don't communicate, which felt, like, really gratifying," she said. "It gave me something that I'd been longing for."

Still, I asked Anne if following the acronym's advice to agree with her mom felt like she was contorting herself again to not upset her mom, as she'd learned to do as a kid. "It felt okay," she told me. "This felt like a way that could preserve her dignity and show empathy for her experience. I had always thought about it as a thing that was making my life miserable. I think I started understanding how miserable she's had to be because of her mental illness." By fibbing and learning to go along with her mom's delusions, Anne was finding a new way to love her mom through her mental illness.

In families, many of us have gotten stuck in entrenched battles over whose version of the story is more correct. Sometimes that's because of mental illness, substance abuse, or trauma in our family's past, or we might just remember things differently. Anne could not convince her mother to see the world the way she did, or talk her mother into being well. But changing the way she talked to her mom—by aligning herself with her and ceding control of the narrative to her mom—created an end run around the battles that had sapped so much of their energy.

For Anne, this new approach of accepting her mother's version of reality preserved their ability to communicate at all. She also had to give up on the idea that, in these moments of crisis, her mother was capable of listening to Anne's point of view. Anne realized she could not stop her mother from getting triggered and having a paranoid episode. Changing the way she communicated also didn't insulate Anne from having to drop everything to help in her mom's next crisis. But it did help Anne see her mom "as another human who is struggling and less as an adversary." And as someone whose brain just worked differently than her own.

When she gave up the fight with her mom over what was real, Anne also accepted the limitations that are always going to be a part of her relationship with her mother. She grieved that, instead of trying to change it.

And she realized that she needed to find other people, chosen family members, to give her the kind of love, support, and ease she didn't have with her mother. "I find other mothers around me. I love the structure and nurturing that I get from older women," she told me. "It's wonderful."

"Our relationship is more important than this disagreement."

Loving our families, when there has been pain and conflict, so often is about letting go. For Anne, she had to give up on the idea that her mother was not sick. Other times, it means surrendering to the idea that a family conflict may never get resolved. When there have been long-held conflicts in families, with deep and real disagreements, coming back together often requires releasing some of the past.

When he was researching family estrangement, sociologist Karl Pillemer found that those family members who were able to come back together did not necessarily have less severe ruptures than the people who couldn't. When families were able to reconnect after estrangement, he found that a common feature was that they gave up on trying to convince each other about what had gone wrong. "People who reconcile describe the experience as letting go of the attempt to have the other person see the past as they saw it," Pillemer said in the *New York Times*.

When Pam Daghlian was a kid growing up in Michigan, she hated her stepfather, George. Until she was eight, she had her mother all to herself. Then one day a bearded man in sunglasses rolled up next to their car. Her mom was intrigued, Pam was scared, "and pretty much from the get-go, he and I did not get along," she admitted.

George was eleven years older than Pam's mom. After his own divorce, he had raised five sons as a single dad with a firm set of rules. When Pam moved into George's house, she resented his stern, disciplinarian style. "Once those rules were my rules, I really started bristling," she said. "It was like this silent war of passive aggression." For example, George had a rule that when you took off sneakers in the house, you had to untie the laces first so you wouldn't damage the backs of the shoes when you were taking them on and off. Pam thought this was ridiculous and ignored it, and then she noticed that her gym shoes were missing from the house. Pam suspected George had taken them, so to get back at him, she hid all of his suspenders. Her shoes magically reappeared.

Part of their tension was normal competitiveness between a kid and her parent's new partner. But Pam was also watching her mother change in ways she didn't understand. They started going to George's conservative Baptist church. "My mom really, really took to it and found something that worked for her." All Pam found in the pews was more confirmation that her mom was abandoning her for a man she did not want to have to deal with. "I was in pretty active hatred of him from ten to eighteen years old," she told me. After she left the house, she went on to major in women's studies and became active in feminist politics. She settled in San Francisco as a life coach, leaving Northern Michigan, and her family there, behind. "We just kind of ignored each other. That lasted through my twenties, through my thirties, through my mid-forties."

Though it was always unspoken, George remembers their relationship the same way. "It was kind of hard feelings there," he told me when I called him to ask about their relationship. When we first talked, he was eight-six, a retired tool-and-die maker in Cadillac, Michigan. "As time went on, we just did not communicate for a long time," George said. "Then her mom got sick."

Pam's mother developed a form of dementia that progressed rapidly. In March 2016, George could no longer care for her at home and they moved her into an assisted living facility. Pam visited more often after her mom started declining, but once she no longer lived with George, Pam had to awkwardly ask if she should still plan to stay at his house. "I don't know that we'd ever been together without her, ever," she observed. "He was, like, 'Of course you're going to stay.'"

George noticed Pam's softening toward him, and he was protective of it. "She started being friendly and accepting us more," he noted, and he didn't want to disrupt that new conviviality. But Pam's mom's deterioration coincided with the 2016 presidential campaign, which inflamed deep divisions among many Americans, including between Pam and George. The same month they moved Pam's mother out of the house, Donald Trump held an enormous rally in town. "It was hard to escape politics and it was hard to escape that we had different politics," Pam said.

Instead of letting politics and their divisions continue to fester and divide them further, "We just decided, let's have a truce; we simply will not talk about anything political or religious," George told me. George was the one who suggested the truce, though Pam had noticed the shift before George announced it in words. George had always had Fox News playing in the background. Without a word, he suddenly never had it on anymore. Pam appreciated the gesture. "Neither of us wanted to mess it up, so we were really careful with each other."

With the truce in place, what was on television became a running joke. Together, they'd watch "forty-seven hours of *Family Feud*," Pam said with a laugh, but whenever she'd leave the house, she'd tell him it was safe to turn on Fox News to have a look. The outside world couldn't be kept out completely, though. "Once in a great while, we'd slip in a little something," George remembered. One night they were watching a presidential debate together, nervously. Finally, Pam remembers, "we both started laughing because we realized that in about thirty minutes or so, no one said a word to each other."

That's when George told her how he was worried that politics would get in the way of their relationship. "He said it first," Pam remembers. "That our relationship was definitely more important than politics." I asked George what prompted him to say that and he said that it wasn't hard. "I just let it out, it's what I feel. You know, I'm not bashful about that," he told me. "It all boils down to values. My value is just to have a friendship and peace with Pam. That was worth more than venting our feelings about politics. And I was the one who said that. But she came right back, that's the way she feels too," he added.

With that assurance in place, they started gingerly talking more about politics, and their disagreements are real and consequential. Because of his faith, George opposes abortion rights and "all the gay rights business," he told me, while one of Pam's first successes as an activist was to charter a fleet of buses to attend an abortion rights rally in Washington, D.C. George thought President Trump was "an oddball" who nevertheless made some great things happen in the country. Pam was disgusted by Trump and considered his rhetoric hateful and dangerous. "I would ask her, 'Why do you think that?' And she would do the same with me," George explained. "I was willing to hear her side of it, no harsh words or anything."

The visits were like that for the next three years. Pam would visit every few months and stay with George for a week or two. Pam tried to concentrate on the listening skills she's honed in her job as a career and life coach. "I really wanted to stay open, so I met him back with my own curiosity," Pam said. "I think he feels safe enough with me to say what he believes and know I'm not going to judge him for it, even if I think he's totally wrong. Which he is, of course." They didn't pretend to agree, and during her regular visits and phone calls their political conversations became more specific and less guarded. Debating sanctuary cities or the benefits of legal immigration was also a nice distraction from the sad reality that had drawn them back together.

"I cannot really tell you how hard it is," George said of his wife's condition. "I think if she had died it would be easier than the way it is now." His wife was no longer verbal, but she still had flashes of recognition during his daily visits, where they just sat together and held hands. "Pam has been so kind to me," George told me. "She's become like a real daughter to me. I learned to just love her to death, and I think she feels the same way. We're very, very close now."

Her mother's illness, Pam said, became "the parallel conversation that really gave us the reason not to fight, because he was sharing with me vulnerable, tenderhearted stuff."

While Pam felt loss and grief because of her mother's dementia, her relationship with George helped her feel less angry. "It's not hard for me in the same way," she admitted to me. For so long, she'd felt like her mom had abandoned her for George, but the trips home during her mother's illness softened her old resentments. She wasn't competing with George anymore; they were experiencing this loss together. "Her dementia, for me, has been this weird and lovely gift that's caused a lot of healing," she said. "It's opened up my whole life. I have forgiven her. I'm not angry anymore. So that's the thing that feels weird to talk to him about."

Saying out loud what they mean to each other, after years of conflict and tension, didn't make their disagreements go away. Those disagreements, though, stopped being deal-breakers.

Pam's mother died in the summer of 2020. Just as they disagreed about politics before, Pam and George didn't agree on the best way to memorialize her in the midst of the Covid-19 pandemic. George and other loved ones in Michigan planned a funeral; Pam told me she didn't feel safe traveling and also didn't feel like it was appropriate to gather.

Pam went on to say, though, that she still treasured the closeness that she and George developed over the many years of visits and their "sweet routine of eating out, making meals together, doting on his dog, and having long talks about life," she wrote in an email the weekend of her mother's funeral. "George and I really have managed to put our bond first. I consider it one of the great achievements of my life, really."

"Can I hear that family story again?"

Pam and George didn't have a warm relationship until she was in her forties and he was in his eighties. They missed a lot of time together, so there was plenty to be curious about in their conversations. But even with family with whom you've been consistently close, asking to hear family stories again can be a way to see each other in more complex, adult ways.

"If a person's behavior doesn't make sense to you, it is because you are missing a part of their context," social psychologist Devon Price wrote. This sentiment certainly applies to family, though because of familiarity, we may be even more quick to assume we should be able to understand certain behavior and choices of family members. When we don't get what they're doing, we judge them, and often tell them how they ought to do things differently.

In my family of origin, I've made those kinds of hurtful judgments, and I've felt the particular sting of feeling misunderstood by the people who are supposed to know me best. As an adult, I've tried to slow down the reaction time when these conflicts rear their heads, and to remember that my confusion is often due to a lack of context—the context being that each member of my family has lived a life apart from me.

That's why it can be valuable to ask to hear family stories again and again. When we first hear family stories, we hear them in relation to ourselves and what they reveal about who we are. Retelling them, and asking for details that have been skipped over, can help us do the crucial work of understanding more about the people in our family, and their decisions that have nothing to do with us.

My parents got married a year and a half after my father's first marriage had ended. He had two daughters with his first wife. My parents then had three more daughters, and we five girls were close as I was growing up, so close that we dispensed early with the term *half*—my two older sisters were and are my sisters. In fact, when I was old enough to realize that not all families were like mine, sometime in early elementary school, I made a decision: when it came time to start my own family, I wanted to marry a divorced father with kids. I wanted my kids to have sisters like I did.

My older sisters felt like a rare gift to me. They are eleven and nine years older than me, the perfect age gap for me to go to them with questions that I never would've asked my parents, equipping me with wisdom that made me more self-assured than my friends who were left to figure things out on their own. From my older sisters I learned the essentials about drugs: pot was okay, mushrooms required a safe space, everything else was potentially too much trouble, and cigarettes were gross. They taught me about music and movies—Bob Marley, Sly and the Family Stone, Deee-Lite, *Kids*, and *Run Lola Run*. And they talked to me about sex. Being in love was good for the first time, my oldest sister instructed me, but even more important was that I should feel ready. They prepared me for being a teenager, a young woman, a feminist. Everything I was going through, they'd done. They were the knowing guides.

Like many a younger sibling, I didn't see my sisters as people who were *also* figuring things out. And they were having to sort through something I never did. I was in college before I really started asking questions about them and their experiences in our family. They told me about their memories of my dad's divorce, and the back-and-forth in court to hammer out a joint custody agreement. My older sisters ended up spending major holidays and summers with us. As a kid, I remember the thrill of their arrival, and then, as they settled in, noticing small tensions I didn't understand. Like when they'd complain about our dad watching sports on TV after working long shifts at the hospital. At the time, I was protective of him, wondering why they weren't easier on him. *He always watches TV to unwind*, I thought. *Who cares?* I didn't understand that when they left their mom's to live with us, they were always sharing my dad's attention: if not with television, then with work or the pack of little sisters hanging around.

To me, my dad's divorce was a settled fact. But for the people who had lived through it in our family, it was and is still part of the evolution of their relationships and understanding of family. When you enter a story that's already started, as all of us do in family, what came before can seem preordained, the result of a static history instead of a series of choices with consequences still unraveling.

The same goes for my parents' decision to marry each other. As a kid, I felt the love story they told us was romantic. My dad said he made a list after his divorce of the qualities he wanted in a partner. He noticed my mom while they worked together at a hospital in Nashville, and she was everything he was looking for. My parents made sense and were meant to be together, this story told me. The list proved it. My dad was sure at the time too. When he asked her to go out, he told her he wasn't looking to just casually date. He wanted to get married again.

When I went through my own divorce, I asked my dad again about that time in his life and that list. I heard for the first time how deep his grief was, grappling with a loss he'd never expected. He was on a retreat, journaling and trying to make sense of what had gone wrong and how he might make it right. I understood then how writing that list also had roots in terror: he desperately wanted to restore order for himself and his daughters and protect them from any more upheaval.

These details scrambled my understanding of my family's origin story, changing it from lore that was set in stone to lived moments that helped me understand my father's choices during a time of great turmoil.

I also asked my mom about that time. I'd always heard how she'd dated a singer-songwriter in Nashville before my dad, which I'd always thought was hopelessly cool, but didn't hear much about their breakup until my ex and I were separating. My mom and the musician were together a long time, and really cared for each other, but came to a point where their lives felt incompatible, with her daytime shifts at the hospital and his nights out playing music. She was dating a rock star, when she really wanted a rock star with a day job.

Then, a few years after my divorce, during the first months of the #MeToo movement and a series of sexual harassment scandals at my company, I asked my parents to tell me more about how the beginning of their relationship went down at the hospital, when he was newly separated and she was fresh out of her relationship.

Where did my father make this grand pronouncement of wanting to date only if she was interested in marriage? In his office, they told me. Was he the boss? Not directly, but my dad was much higher up in the hospital hierarchy and my mom knew it. He was also nine years older than she was. Forty-five years ago, my dad's directness put my mom on the spot in a way that a modern HR office would flag, and I told them so. My mom nodded. It was a little overwhelming, she allowed with a smile. It must have been a lot to take in for a young woman who was just three years out of college, living on her own with her first set of houseplants.

My dad's proposal wasn't just about taking up with him; it also meant my mother would become an immediate stepmother when she was in her mid-twenties. Did she know the first thing about kids? I asked. No, my mom explained, but after their first date, she was under no illusions. My dad thought it was a good idea to invite my mom to a children's science museum with both my sisters, on a busy weekend afternoon. The younger one had a major tantrum and my dad had to take her outside. My mom described being left alone in the planetarium with my oldest sister, then six, as they both awkwardly and wordlessly stared up at the stars.

My parents married within a year of their first date. Both of them were coming off of experiences that upended all they knew, and instead of flinching, they decided to go through whatever was next together. My parents had to figure out a way to deal with a family that was coming together, apart, and back together in ways they didn't anticipate. So did my older sisters. I think back on the pictures of them from my parents' wedding album, in dresses handmade by my mom's mother, a nice older woman they'd just met. I realize how different family had looked for them a year before, and then there they were, in a small church off a rural highway, with one side of the wedding party filled with total strangers.

It was the mid-seventies; divorce rates in the United States were climbing to their peak in the late seventies and early 1980s. Lots of parents and kids were going through divorce, with a lot fewer resources and models for how to do it well. These people—my dad the groom, his little kids, their nervous stepmom—didn't know what they were doing, but there they were, doing it together, as a new family.

As I've gotten older, remarried, and become a mother myself to two little girls, I try to pan the camera around my parents' wedding scene to understand all the dynamics unfolding in my family before I showed up. It's remarkable to me how obvious this is, and how long it's taken me to do it. Asking questions about well-worn family stories reveals edges and tensions that were tamped down in the first versions I heard as a child. As my perspective moves around, and I hear those stories over and over again, my understanding deepens. I learn that *my* version of my family is not all that my family is. Each time, I see more clearly that every family is made up of individuals, with their own version of a family's story, as they separate and come back together.

In family relationships, time sands down the edges of conflicts, hurt, and misunderstanding. Our first reactions can evolve into more measured and generous interpretations. But years can also fly by in family conflicts, without any hint of movement toward resolution. So, when it comes to hard family conversations, an enormous amount hinges on timing. We have to be attentive to the slow shifts in our long-term relationships, and be willing to call them into conversation when gaps begin to yawn.

That's why Yesi Ortiz had to change the way she talked to her sister's children as they grew into adults: instead of telling them how to be, she now had to listen to what they needed. Similarly, Adrian came to realize during a time of crisis that he couldn't have the kinds of hard conversations that he needed within his family. He stepped out of his role as a happy participant in a large, rollicking extended family and sought help beyond what his loved ones could offer.

Such decisions to shake up our approach in our familial relationships don't happen all at once. As Desiree Akhavan described, incremental conversations helped her family members establish boundaries and make room for updates as they readjusted their relationships with one another. "I think taking space is a really helpful thing if you feel like you can't define who you are or build the relationship you want," Desiree told me. "We have our roles that we slip into and it's easy to blame your family for keeping you there, but I think we also keep ourselves there."

In families, the passage of time also reveals the qualities and challenges of our families that are unlikely to change. For Anne, understanding her mother's reality meant also accepting her mother's inability to observe reality as Anne knew it. As painful as that was, it was also necessary. To engage in difficult family conversations does not always mean that we have to agree or forgive. Accepting the limitations of the people in our family is both realistic and compassionate.

There are also cases where our family members cannot love us in the ways we need, when they cause more harm whenever we try to reconnect. In these scenarios, loving at a distance may be all that's achievable. It's possible to heal such relationships over time, as we saw with Pam Daghlian and her stepfather, George, who had no illusions about how they disagreed but made a concerted effort to focus toward where they connected and away from where they didn't. Still, this isn't always viable. In the end it's okay to accept that family can't give us everything and to seek out other avenues toward the comfort and support we need.

In adulthood, our family relationships mature when we figure out how to see our family members, and to be seen by them, as individual people. One of the most effective ways of doing this is to revisit family stories. Asking different family members for their own accounts of the same story has let my vantage point skip around in time and space, and has helped me complicate my understanding of my family members' experiences. This offers a simple way to hear that your family members each have different relationships to one another—and don't solely exist in relationship to you. Hearing all those perspectives doesn't mean agreeing with everything that's happened or forgiving everyone's mistakes. But it lets you catch a glimpse of a fundamental truth about the people we come from: that a family is a bunch of individuals, each doing what they can, jostling for space in one moment, then holding each other tight the next.

It's a mess, but it's also a whole. And when we make the effort in hard conversations within our families, we can come to understand that more clearly, so that the dirt and dust of our worst days don't cloud out the warmth and light of our best days.

Identity

I was the only student in my class at Stanford from West Virginia, which I didn't expect to feel all that important, until I had to keep explaining where I was from. Anyone who had a foggy sense of the state pictured backwoods shacks and dust-covered coal miners, but more often, people didn't have any idea of West Virginia at all. So I had to figure out how to make my own introduction to the place. I grasped for the right phrases to express my affection, without glossing over her flaws or being overly sentimental. There's a generous and a not-so-generous way to explain my state's history, beginning with the way it cleaved itself from Virginia during the Civil War and what it became after.

At home, we knew West Virginia's shortcomings well, so we didn't need to say them out loud. There's the high rate of poverty, the poor health outcomes, the overarching perilousness that comes from relying on dangerous, extractive industries. I grew up in an affluent neighborhood in the capital city, but I still could see how much our fate was determined by people who didn't live among us: out-of-state landowners, Wall Street investors, executives who ran the chemical, coal, and gas companies—and later, the pharmaceutical companies hawking pain pills. Most of these people were not looking out for us, we suspected. When we did attract notice from outsiders, we had finely attuned antennae that picked up on any derision or paternalism in their tone. We were used to being a joke in West Virginia, or the destination of church groups on spring break mission trips. We are protective of our home, and accustomed to feeling let down when people don't get it.

This makes for a close-knit sense of identity, even with people you otherwise vehemently disagree with. Together, this is *our* underdog state, and we're proud of her. I can still belt out the song of her fifty-five counties. I thrill when national broadcasters say something nice about Mountaineer sports teams. And if anyone ever mentions someone famous who I know is from West Virginia, I'm going to tell you. Bill Withers! Jennifer Garner! Steve Harvey! Brad Paisley! Mary Lou Retton! Katherine Johnson! They are us too!

Still, as ingrained as this cultural identity was in me, I just thought *everybody* was like this about their state. Only when I got to Stanford and took in the gleaming opulence of Silicon Valley did I realize that not everyone grows up in a place where *snob* is one of the worst insults you could hurl at someone. I'd never been around so much wealth, talk about wealth, and the possibility for *more* wealth. I didn't know what an IPO was when I showed up on campus; someone had to explain the reference when it came up in a freshman orientation skit.

Like a lot of dimensions of identity, I didn't know that *any* of my upbringing was unique until I was the odd one out. And with that came the realization of how uncertain and ungrounded I felt away from home. So I doubled down. I listened to bluegrass music in my dorm room, asked professors to let me do guided readings on Appalachian history, and when I graduated, I headed back to West Virginia. I had no real plan, except to go back to where I fit. I started my journalism career in West Virginia, got married, bought a house.

And then, five years later, like generations of West Virginians before and after me, I left again to chase down opportunity elsewhere. This too is woven into our identity. The unofficial anthem for our state, John Denver's "Take Me Home, Country Roads," is sung from the point of view of a singer who's left home and can't help missing it.

When word started to get around town that I was moving away, a buddy of mine pulled over when he saw me walking on a sidewalk. He rolled down his window and yelled, "Quitter!" He smiled, and also knew that it would sting. It still stings.

But even as I moved away, I carried with me the many parts of myself that come straight from West Virginia. I built a belief system around reflexively looking out for the underdog. This has shaped my journalism and my values. I understood how being dismissed and talked over can curdle into resentment. I have some of that resentment myself, in the way I still bristle when I hear self-satisfied elites talking about how everyone else ought to live. The West Virginian in me is always trying to listen instead, and to pick up on what I'm missing. I see this as part of the necessary work of building back something essential, some kind of unity and understanding, in our angry, divided society.

Of course, even as I find something distinctive about where I come from, as far as identities go, being a white, well-off West Virginian is low stakes. It doesn't come with the painful history of hate and injustice that is embedded in being Black or gay, or any number of marginalized identities in America. I'm educated, financially stable, and can pick when to reveal my West Virginia-ness. I can slide back into my accent with someone suspicious of my coastal media profile. Or, I can deemphasize that part of me and present as just another white woman in journalism who's reading the right books, watching the right TV shows, and up on all the in-jokes on Twitter. I have the luxury of being able to shape-shift, to anticipate and maneuver around a lot of the negative assumptions of how I might be read. As Isabel Wilkerson wrote in *Caste,* her sweeping book about social hierarchy, racism, and identity, "If you can act your way out of it, then it is class, not caste."

That also means that, because of my identity, I am able to listen to the frustrations and resentments of many in America without fearing that I will become the target of their misdirected anger. Plenty of people don't have that option, because they're not white, or English-speaking, or straight-appearing. Anyone at all whose differences can be contorted by prejudice doesn't have the option to slide out of view. Living with that fact presents a whole different set of questions when it comes to hard conversations about identity: Do I insist on my dignity in this conversation and brace for the response? If I disagree, or stand up for myself, what are all the ways I might be threatened? Am I safe? This is a fundamentally different exercise.

Liam Lowery, a housing attorney in the Bronx, told me that he is often navigating these questions in conversations about his identity. Liam is a trans man whom I first met when I interviewed him on the show; when we spoke again for this book, he told me he tries to approach identity conversations with openness while staying attuned to what he calls a "trip wire." When crossed, that signal blares out: *Time to go. Gotta cut my losses and get out of here.*

Liam told me that when he's talking about being trans with someone who may not know much about gender identity, he tries to be clear about what his objective is for the conversation. Is the primary motivation in that moment to speak truth to power, or does he want to tread more gingerly to make a connection? In the first case, when he's calling something out, he described, "I'm creating a record, to declare *this is wrong and here's why*." In the second scenario, "You make other decisions, so they buy in and engage." That kind of conversation requires him to meet people where they are, instead of the other way around. "Sometimes you have to create a shared language that's maybe not the truest," Liam said.

Specificity and nuance can strangely get in the way of finding a common vocabulary, so he's always asking himself, *Which objective is more important today?* This dynamic is common to many identity conversations. Welcoming someone in takes time and effort. Sometimes you have the wherewithal, and you come out feeling more understood. Sometimes, it's not worth it.

———

A friend once compared the challenge of identity dynamics to walking into a family reunion as an outsider. You are poorly equipped to really understand what is happening. You don't have the history, the knowledge, and the trained-through-life experience to see all the dynamics. You might think the great-uncle is polite and perfectly nice, but not catch his passive-aggressive comment or the hurtful dart embedded in this joke. You won't know what it means that the aunt is drinking tonight or the older sister is standing in the corner, a little quiet. To explain all this, to get you caught up on the story, takes work and, often, more than a little awkwardness.

Throughout this chapter, when I talk about identity, I'm focusing on the broad categories that connect and divide us—race, ethnicity, gender, sexuality, class, religion, disability—and all the hard sorts of personal conversations that derive from these collective identities. For the purposes here, I'm also putting a priority on how to navigate these conversations in our interpersonal relationships—whether among colleagues, friends, or family. These are the sorts of hard conversations that come up in team meetings at work, or around the dinner table with family, in which we are listening to how others see the world and asking whether they can hear how our experience is different.

Handling these conversations poorly can severely damage, or even ruin, a relationship. When we assume too much about what knowledge we share, or leap into the fray to compare experiences that half rhyme, we can throw the whole outcome into jeopardy. Identity conversations are about creating space for differences— differences that are layered with power and pain—in the hopes of creating a feeling of connection, or at least a sense of peace with the distance that remains. You are ideally listening and speaking in a way that seeks to honor your conversation partner's dignity and experience, and your own. This doesn't mean shying away from clumsiness, though. Fear of saying the wrong thing often stops a needed identity conversation before it ever starts. Fumbling over the right words can be a crucial part of navigating real differences, so long as it follows from listening openly and honestly.

Part of what is so hard about identity conversations is they are at once deeply personal and sweeping in their scope. We are often comparing different versions of reality, and tracing dividing lines that mark historical legacies of privilege and visibility—who has counted and who "fit in," who is on the outside, and how that is changing. We have to grapple with the big, broad categories that we're slotted into, and how they interact with the ways we see ourselves. Engaging honestly with a subject like racism means facing down centuries of injustice, and inequalities that have been deeply embedded in our society since long before we were born. At the same time, these exchanges are immediate and intimate. "The truth is that nothing is impersonal when it comes to racism, or the will to subjugate," Hilton Als wrote in the *New Yorker* in the weeks after George Floyd's death. "Every act of racism is a deeply personal act with an end result: the unmooring diminishment of the person who is the target."

The stakes are incredibly high, and they cut straight to our deepest sense of self. "I live knowing that whatever my blackness means to me can be at odds with what it means to certain white observers, at any moment," Wesley Morris wrote in the *New York Times Magazine* in 2015. "So I live with two identities: mine and others' perceptions of it." This is what W. E. B. Du Bois called "double-consciousness" in 1897, "this sense of always looking at one's self through the eyes of others, of measuring one's soul by the tape of a world that looks on in amused contempt and pity." Of course, if the broader world tends to see your identity as typical or paradigmatic, then this double-consciousness doesn't function in the same way at all.

This means that, depending on who you are, the workloads in conversations around identity are different. Those with the least power and privilege have often had to carry the burden of explaining the costs and historical consequences of dividing, overpowering, and excluding people based on identity. "We are here because you were there," declared Ambalavaner Sivanandan, the British novelist of Sri Lankan descent, in the 1980s, to help white Britons understand how colonization led to a multiracial, multiethnic United Kingdom.

For people who don't fit into normative categories of gender or sexuality, for people of color, for immigrants, for anyone with a disability, this is not new information. *Marginalization* is one term often used for these identities, but another way to think about it is in terms of belonging. This framing creates more space for the movement between contexts: You may be marginalized in one setting and empowered in another. Noticing when and how that's changed can tell you a lot about how identity functions in your life. Where do you belong? Among whom? Who belongs where you belong, and who is an outlier?

When you put in the work to notice where you and others feel belonging, and where you feel cast out, there is a fundamental shift in how you can approach conversations about identity. You are listening for places of connection, where you may come together, what you can build on. The law professor john a. powell, who directs the Othering & Belonging Institute at UC Berkeley, argues that a focus on belonging creates an important distinction from *inclusion*, a current buzzword for bringing in more marginalized voices. "Inclusion suggests you're joining something that's already there," he said in a speech in 2020, like a party where the menu is already set, along with the music playlists and the guest list. "Whereas belonging suggests that you're co-creating the thing you belong to. You're *co-creating* it. So now all of a sudden, instead of it being my party, it's our party.

"That's good," powell said. "It's also work."

For people who are used to fitting in—like, say, a straight, white, financially stable, married mom, albeit one from West Virginia—how you identify and how you are identified can feel one and the same. That is, you are missing a dimension of consciousness, so that when you do feel yourself profiled or categorized or summed up in a way that doesn't feel authentic to your own self-concept, it feels wrong and unfamiliar. What it really is, though, is a way the world works that you haven't been forced to notice. I haven't known the full humiliation of having my individuality stamped out because of someone else's categorization, or of feeling like who I am is being misread beyond the bounds of my own power. What I lack in firsthand experience, I have to make up for in listening. The type of listening that doesn't jump in, and doesn't immediately layer on my personal experiences, excuses, assurances, or apologies.

When I go into a hard conversation about identity, I also have to gird myself for some new realizations about how my blind spots and indifference have hurt others, and to be prepared to feel more unsettled than I was before I started the conversation. Karena Montag, a therapist in California's East Bay who runs restorative justice trainings, told me she asks groups at the beginning of sessions "to expect and accept a lack of closure." A lack of resolution, in fact, indicates progress, because talking about identity underscores the limits of our ability to simply intuit an understanding of others. You have to ask. You have to experience the weightlessness of not knowing. Another reason for the lack of closure in hard identity conversations is that a single conversation won't upend patterns of oppression. Just like conversations about money don't flatten the material differences between us, honest conversations about racism don't cure centuries of material inequality. But more nuance and detail lead us to more truth and understanding, and real political changes can only follow from understanding.

And so these conversations about identity are not one-and-done. After you've had hard conversations about identity, privilege, and the personal limits to your point of view, conflicts about identity will flare up again. The pain in these moments can be acute and surprising—*How can you know me and not know this?* They make us realize with a jolt that we're not as aligned with one another as we thought. In these situations, we have to back up, reset, and go over basic facts of our lives and how our society works—which may seem strange. But the root issue is that we've experienced these facts differently, or failed to absorb them in the first place. And when we have the hard conversation, with the sincere intention to learn and listen, we come away with a fuller understanding of the world we live in together, and what it is like to navigate it from a full range of perspectives. Talking alone won't diminish the force of marginalization or undo historical injustices, but it can make us feel less isolated, more understood, and ready to work to create a world where more of us feel like we belong.

"All I'm asking for is understanding."

I first met Anpo Kuwa Win in a tipi in Wyoming, where she was spending the day with the doorway open to answer tourists' questions during a powwow.

As she sat surrounded by a constant flow of white people, I was impressed by the way she talked. The questions tourists asked were simple and wide-ranging—about everything from the history of powwows and the different styles of dancing to the role of nature in indigenous cultures in America. She dispensed with some quickly. "Actually, I think that's a very stereotypical question," she began, in response to a German tourist eager to hear about her people's particularly close relationship to the land. "That erases our humanness. Some of us litter!" she said, laughing, and then went on to describe cultural practices and demographics of Native people today living on and off tribal land.

When she and I talked later, I asked her why she spent a summer afternoon answering the questions of visitors who knew so little of her people's history. "My mother volunteered me," she said. "Actually, it's my great-grandfather's fault." Her great-grandfather, Benjamin Franklin Marable, died when Anpo was still in high school—at 105 or 106, no one knew for sure. He was one of the last surviving members of the *Wild West Show*, the traveling variety show that Buffalo Bill Cody toured around the United States and Europe from the late nineteenth century into the early twentieth. The show created many of the now-familiar mythologies of the American West frontier. Anpo's great-grandfather acted out the parts Buffalo Bill assigned him, but he also considered it an important responsibility to represent Native American people to white audiences. "You have to educate them," he told his great-granddaughter, "because these are the people who will make decisions that will affect your children."

That's why, one hundred years later, Anpo patiently answers tourists' questions inside the tipi. Every summer, the powwow is held on the grounds of the Center of the West museum in Cody, so families driving through on their trips to Yellowstone National Park mingle with indigenous families who gathered to join in singing and dance competitions, wearing brightly colored dresses of animal hides, feathers, and beads. "One of the reasons you sit in the tipi is to make people see that those of us dancing are the same as those of us over here walking around," she explained. She wants to make sure the tourists don't just take in the powwow as a spectacle and leave without a more nuanced understanding of Native Americans today. "We're just as important when we take off the beads and feathers."

Anpo lives on the Wind River Reservation in Wyoming, where the Eastern Shoshone and Northern Arapaho tribes now share land despite rivalries going back thousands of years. She's a middle school librarian in the reservation school district, and her job title includes the term *cultural facilitator*. She told me, "Building relationships is the biggest part of my job," whether with coworkers (most white) who've arrived on the reservation to help the kids, or with the kids from different and often multiple tribal backgrounds who've landed in classrooms together. When she's talking about identity, her approach differs depending on her audience, on whether the person she is talking to is Native or not.

Anpo was born on the Pine Ridge Indian Reservation in South Dakota and is still an enrolled member of the Lakota tribe. She moved to Wyoming when she was three years old, and she's felt like an outsider on the reservation there. She's now middle-aged and lives with her mother on the reservation in Wyoming, with her adult daughter's and son's families living nearby.

Other Native people on the reservation know that she's Lakota, because when they introduce themselves to each other, they begin with their tribal affiliation. But when she meets non-Native people, she said it's simpler to gloss over all that and just says she's Native. "Why spend another fifteen minutes of your time explaining the tribal background to people who still won't understand?" Every day, Anpo toggles between these two ways of being: finding connection with Native people despite their very different tribal histories and personal affiliations, and then explaining herself to people who know very little indigenous history and see Native people as all the same.

When I visited her on the Wind River Reservation a few weeks after we first met, she drove me to the grave site of Sacagawea, the Shoshone woman who became an essential guide and interpreter for Meriwether Lewis and William Clark's expedition across the western side of the North American continent. I told Anpo that I'm related to Lewis on my father's side and that I wasn't sure how to feel about this, since his chronicles created the ground-work for white expansion through the American West, and his family—my family—enslaved people on their land in Virginia.

"Well, if it makes you feel better, I have a relative who killed twenty-three white men!" she said with a laugh.

It was a classically awkward exchange about identity. I was trying to demonstrate my self-awareness about my whiteness and history, and she picked up on my guilt. She made a joke to ease the social tension that also underscored, yes, we are on different sides of this thing.

"I've never thought the world was fair. I always thought it was unjust," she told me as we sat in her car at an intersection beside a big general store on the reservation, which she told me is owned by white people and sells Native blankets to passing tourists. Anpo showed me the stone guard towers on the perimeter, where the federal government used to keep watch on Native people who lived there. She told me the history of Native children being sent away from their families to be educated in boarding schools and pointed out the many churches that missionaries have built on the land over the years. "The Native part of me is always like, *Goddamn, why didn't you stay in your own community and preach to people like you? Why did you feel the need to come here and foist your religion on us?*" she mused about missionaries on the reser-vation, past and present. "But then, on the other hand, it's like,

215

Man, you guys were brave! Stupid, but brave. You came all the way west. You know, you didn't know where you were."

These outsiders are part of her everyday life on the reservation. At work, she routinely has to help her white coworkers understand the children they work with. As she's explaining life on the reservation, and which assumptions and blind spots of theirs are harmful and why, she told me, she thinks of how she would explain it to a toddler. "You can't just tell a toddler, *don't touch the stove*. You have to explain that they can't touch the stove because it's hot and they'll get burned," she said. "Otherwise, they'll just want to touch the stove again." She has taught her colleagues about the sacredness of water to many tribes, to warn against anyone thoughtlessly wasting it or throwing around water bottles. She's had to tell teachers not to touch a child's head without permission, because the head is sacred to the Arapaho—and also because that would be presumptuous and rude. She explains Native history, generational poverty, and inherited trauma.

This takes work since, in taking on the role of "explainer," she's tasked with representing all Native people. She reads history about indigenous people and the American government, to understand the roots of the structures that make life on the reservation different from life off of it. She's honed the way she talks about who she is and who Native people are, in such a way that she can feel heard. "My biggest problem is, I'll be honest with you, white people don't listen!" she said. "They are constantly thinking about what they're going to say, what their response is, what their defense is, or what their excuse is."

Anpo doesn't want excuses. She doesn't want pushback. She just wants to be able to communicate what her experience as a Native American woman has been. She wants to tell her family stories, recount what she has learned living on the Wind River Reservation, describe what it's like to teach there, all while not managing anyone's reactions. "It's like, wait a minute, I'm not talking about you! I'm not asking for anything from you. All I'm asking you for is understanding, and that's not a hard thing to give me," she said. "Goddammit, that's what I need."

As a Native educator of Native students, she also feels an immense responsibility to help them understand the traditions and history they come from, and what it means for their experience in the world. Anpo considers it part of her job to prepare young people on the reservation for the challenges they will face, because of who they are and the difficulties facing their communities. She's explicit with preteen girls about the high rates of sexual assault against Native American women. More than 56 percent of Native women have experienced sexual violence in their lifetimes, and Native women also experience higher rates of physical violence than women of other races. Stranger rape and sex trafficking are threats, Anpo tells the girls, from white men wandering on the reservation, looking for victims. Most indigenous women who are sexually assaulted, more than two-thirds, are victimized by white or non-Native men, and there are also high rates of child abuse. Anpo tells the girls she herself is a survivor of childhood sexual abuse. She will say to three young girls, "There are three of you here. One, two, three," she'll say. "That means there's a possibility that two of you will be sexually assaulted. Be careful. Be aware."

To boys, she explains how the criminal justice system treats Native men. She tells them about high rates of incarceration: Native men are incarcerated at four times the rate of white men, and are also much more likely to be killed by police than white men. And, she tells them, if they are arrested on tribal land, they may end up in federal court and face stiffer penalties. Anpo tells them about her son, who was arrested on a reservation days after his eighteenth birthday with three ounces of marijuana. He was indicted on federal charges and faced up to thirty years, and eventually pled out and served six years in federal prison, moving between facilities many states away from her and their family. He's out now, but he was changed by the brutality and violence inside prison. "It ruined his life," she said.

She wants them to understand that their room for error is smaller because they are Native. She wants them to be prepared and to situate their personal difficulties within the long history of their people. And, Anpo tells them, they have reason to be proud because they have endured, despite this history. "You are here because someone ran faster. You are here because someone hid. You are here because someone survived. And if they didn't, you wouldn't be here. Honor their sacrifice. Honor their survival," she told me she often says. "Learn your family history, learn your language, learn where your last name comes from."

Her conversations about identity are direct and honest as she navigates between two very distinct audiences. When she's talking to someone who is not Native, she might be the only Native person they've met and she feels the weight and responsibility of representing what it means to be Native today. It's an unfair burden, and also an opportunity. She needs them to understand that the realities they notice are the result of the long history of laws, policies, war, and violence that have treated Native people like they shouldn't belong. She peppers these interactions with jokes, but she wants it all to sink in: *There are things you do not understand; let me explain.*

For Native kids, those who share the identity of being indigenous in the United States, Anpo wants them to know the insults they hear and the diminished opportunities before them are not because of anything they have personally done. They will have to deal with those realities regardless, but they can draw from their shared identity to remind themselves of their strength and purpose. And she shares her personal experiences with painful and unjust realities in Native American communities, so they know they have someone to turn to and aren't alone.

About a year after she drove me around the reservation, I saw Anpo again when she was back doing tipi education duty at the annual powwow in Cody, Wyoming. I asked her over for pizza afterward, and she agreed. (Our text exchange: "Do you eat meat?" Response: "We're Indians, all we eat is meat.")

I talked to her about the moments from our conversations about identity that stuck out for me. I reminded her that she'd blamed her great-grandfather for her feeling of obligation to educate white people about Native people, when he said that those were the people who held the power for the fortunes of Native children and grand-children. Yes, Anpo replied, that was what her great-grandfather had said, but hearing me say that she and other Native people didn't have the power to control their destinies felt off. That wasn't quite right, she told me. Hearing me sum it up that way missed something essential about the power of deeply knowing and holding on to your identity in the face of hostility and violence.

In conversations about identity, it matters who is saying what. Coming from me, a white person, it sounded like I was diminishing the choices and possibilities for Native people.

A few days later, she sent me a long text. "I've been thinking a lot about power," she wrote.

She described driving across Wyoming the day before, pulling over for a bathroom break, and coming out of a rest stop to see a man helping an older woman out of a red truck. They were strangers but she instantly felt a sense of recognition. "The only thing that we knew about each other was that we were Native and somehow fate had brought us to this ridiculously ugly rest stop in the middle of Nowhere, Wyoming." They smiled at each other and exchanged pleasantries. She learned they were from New Mexico. She told them her father was Isleta, a tribe from near what is now Albuquerque. They wished each other safe travels. And then Anpo wrote to me that she drove away:

> In that moment, I realized that even through all the horrible struggles and terrible things that have happened, it's so good to see someone that looks like you and to be able to recognize each other and know that there are other people out there who survived. Therein lies our true power, our ability to not just survive, but to adapt and even thrive.
>
> One of my mother's greatest gifts to me was the love of words, books, and poems. One of my favorite poems she shared with me when I was going through an absolutely terrible time in my life was "Invictus," which I know some people love to hate, but as I was driving down that lonesome road, the sky was suddenly bluer, the grass greener, the air lighter, and I thanked the creator for my unconquerable soul.

"What does it mean to continue to push?"

When I first met Anpo as she was answering questions from passing tourists, she was getting paid by the museum hosting the powwow on its grounds. But as she told me, she is always doing the work of explaining her identity, labor that often feels unequal, emotionally draining, and maddeningly predictable. Gauging whether and when to start a conversation about identity is a common, daily exercise.

When it comes to identity, the people lower down on the social hierarchy are usually the ones tasked with this calculus. "I have to figure out first, is this the fight I'll fight today? Do I want to go do this? Can I let it go today?" Meshea Poore told me. She's a Black woman in her forties, from the same small city in West Virginia that I am. Meshea is an attorney, a former legislator, and a top administrator at West Virginia University. In professional settings, she is very often the only Black person in the room. She could not be more practiced at talking about identity, because when anything regarding race or difference comes up, she's used to all heads turning to her.

"I talk about it all the time," she told me. "You're expected to carry the mantle for everything. I'm supposed to be the Black voice for everything. I'm supposed to be able to be the champion of every single issue and talk to a room full of white men or sometimes white women who don't always get it. So you get very comfortable in that space," she said, then stopped. "You don't get comfortable in that space, but you have to *own* that space. You don't have room for discomfort because the work still has to get done."

Everything she communicates has layers: *What do I want to say? How do I say it in a way that will be heard? How might they react?* Like Anpo, she has to approach these conversations like a parent who's trying to manage the blowback from a child: *How do I best convey disappointment, or ask for a change in behavior, without getting sidetracked with a total meltdown?* "So my thing is I always have to relate. You find commonalities. *You want to talk about flowers, my mama grows flowers! You know, I've gone fishing!"* she said. "You begin to let people know you're human." She has to balance the dual objectives of showing that she's approachable and that she deserves to be heard.

That doesn't mean she's always up for the labor of arguing she's worthy of dignity. Sometimes Meshea just lets insults go by. "Once you put energy into that fight, it dictates your level of peace for the day," she told me. "Because it's emotional. It's personal. It's real." She knows that whenever she brings up a critique of something that's been said or overlooked, she will reflexively be told that what was said wasn't intended to be racist and that the person who said it isn't racist. Then Meshea will have to respond in a way that will cut through the defensiveness. "You spend more time trying to get them comfortable to even hear what you're saying," she said. "It amazes me that you are the person who was originally offended, but by stating the offense, the person who has offended, now is offended! And now you've got to make them feel comfortable! It's completely exhausting because the issue is never addressed. Because you're now addressing *their* offense."

When she chooses to speak up, she has learned that she can't be subtle or mealymouthed, and that means tamping down her first wave of emotions. Instead, Meshea analyzes the response she expects to get if she calls someone out, so she'll be ready with another tactic if she meets a defensive reaction. She's both having a conversation and noticing the conversation as it unfolds, gauging how much it fits the patterns she has come to know intimately. "What does it mean to continue to push? What do you have to do to make them see it? Do you have to pull back your words? Do you need to change your words to get them to see it because it's that important? Or do you revisit it another time? You just have to gauge that."

Meshea told me about sitting on a statewide committee to advise the governor on judicial appointments. The committee was made up of some attorneys like Meshea and people from other fields. Including one guy in particular, "a white man with white hair," who didn't know Meshea from her time as a legislator or the leader of the state bar association. At one meeting, as an offhand comment, he said something about Confederate monuments not being a big deal. "I heard it, but my mind must have said, *Not today*," Meshea said, laughing. "Because to this day I could not tell you what that man said. I had already tuned him out." She did notice the room go quiet after he said it and sensed that she was being watched afterward. In fact, another white man in the meeting told her later that she handled the moment very well.

At their next scheduled meeting, Meshea was the first member of the committee to arrive. Confederate Statue Man followed in shortly after. "I said good morning, and he responded." And then, as Meshea watched, he walked out of the room to try to find a staff person for the venue to ask if he had the right room because no one was there yet. She heard someone say to him, "Meshea's in there." He walked back in, "and before I knew it, I said, 'I said good morning to you. You must've thought I work here.'" She watched it register on his face. "My response triggered something in him. He was shamed, but also he took offense."

Still, he sat down next to her at the meeting table, turned to her, and asked what she did. She told him about working on diversity and inclusion at the university. "And he said, 'Diversity, huh?' And I thought, *Oh, here we go . . .*" But they kept talking. Their interaction prompted the white man with white hair to reflect on his experiences with racism. He told Meshea about growing up in the 1950s and being in a public school as it integrated after *Brown v. Board of Education*, and Meshea described how the challenges of her job varied from campus to campus around West Virginia. He told her that his daughter worked in urban education and Meshea told him about the implicit bias test from Harvard, how taking it helps people recognize the negative and positive associations they carry around with them about people depending on their perceived race and how they look.

"I told him he should take it and he typed it in his phone," Meshea said. "By the end of our conversation, I knew his daughter's name. And I said, 'I promise, if you take the test and tell your daughter, she'll be very impressed with you.' We joked the whole rest of the meeting. Now, I'm not saying he's my best friend, but we have an opportunity," she continued. "Had we both not stepped out of ourselves and our personal issues and sat in that space and talked, I never would've been able to say that."

It turned into a warm social exchange. But it started with Meshea holding her ground and pointing out his insult. The meeting before, she didn't want to have to be the person calling out his Confederate monument comments, especially in a room full of others who also could have done the work. But this time she wasn't going to just let it pass, especially when this encounter was between just the two of them and so was harder to ignore. It wasn't a decision, necessarily; it was a reflex after his snub. She couldn't predict or control his reaction, but on this day she had to say something out loud.

Put another way, the calculus can be: *What do I need to do today to take care of myself?* Speaking up is necessary, but not necessary in every situation. For Meshea, some days, when she hears a stray comment about Confederate monuments, she puts it in the mental file and moves on. Other days, she registers that she heard something, makes it known she noticed, but does not take up the mantle of the teaching and feelings management that follows. (You can tell people to do some googling.) Other times, she dives in. "You have to figure out a way to articulate it in a way that will get what you need to get," Meshea said.

Speaking up is both empowering *and* taxing. Some days, she just has to say, "Not today."

"Niceness has nothing to do with it!"

For Anpo and Meshea, "hard" conversations about identity are hard because, when they start talking to someone different from them, they're wondering, *Are you going to hear me or not?* These doubts for them are routine and predictable. Their familiarity makes them all the more wearying.

For people who are part of dominant identity groups—white people, straight people, people without disabilities—conversations across identity differences become hard for a totally different set of reasons. For them—or depending on how you identify, for us—being asked to notice the everyday insults, built-in biases, and long-standing injustices can feel like indictments for crimes you didn't knowingly commit.

So, defensiveness can come up, or *white fragility*, as anti-racist educator Robin DiAngelo calls it: that urge to deny the way privilege and advantage shape lives. Or you may notice the opposite reaction welling up as you register harms and injustice you previously hadn't: a frantic urge to get this all fixed! For people in dominant identity categories, because institutions, laws, and social conventions were designed to keep you personally comfortable, you have a certain faith in your ability to change these systems to suit your evolving worldview.

Writer Erin Aubrey Kaplan, a Black woman, watched this play out in her marriage with her white husband, Alan. "Our different upbringings made for different outlooks," she wrote in the *New York Times* in 2018, as she mourned Alan's death. "In Alan's privilege he expected change; in my non-privilege, I expected struggle. For all his wokeness, he couldn't escape his American sense of entitlement, and sometimes I watched it from the outside with a kind of bewilderment, even admiration."

For people in dominant identity categories, having hard conversations about identity requires that you first notice unsettling truths about power, unfairness, and injustice, and how these threads are part of everything, from our institutions to our interpersonal interactions. Mixed in with righteous indignation and defensiveness, there can also be a kind of shameful turning inward. Let me encourage you to linger there. That impulse to slow down is important. You need to take some time to incorporate all of this into your self-image and the story you tell about yourself.

That's the model set by Peggy McIntosh, a researcher at Wellesley who studies privilege. In an academic paper in 1988, she made a list of the ways her social ease and professional success were positively influenced by her whiteness. She did not coin the term *white privilege*—she credits W. E. B. Du Bois with conceptualizing it in the 1930s when he wrote of "the [additional] psychological wage" given to even poor whites—but she described how being white made her life easier. She conveyed this by making it personal:

1. I can, if I wish, arrange to be in the company of people of my race most of the time . . .

10. I can be fairly sure of having my voice heard in a group in which I am the only member of my race . . .

17. I can talk with my mouth full and not have people put this down to my color . . .

21. I am never asked to speak for all the people of my racial group . . .

32. My culture gives me little fear about ignoring the perspectives and powers of people of other races . . .

34. I can worry about racism without being seen as self-interested or self-seeking . . .

And so on, until she had a list of forty-six ways her life had been shaped by her identity. "Exemption from discrimination is as important and organic to the problem of racism as discrimination is," she told me when I called her at her home in Massachusetts. "Most white people have not been made aware of our identities, except as the norm."

Peggy began thinking about privilege at work during a series of monthly feminist seminars at Wellesley that she led for a few years with a group of professors, women and men, from many institutions. She noticed that every year, after they had sat together and discussed all the evidence that sidelining women's voices was a problem, especially in the curriculum, there started to be a predictable turn. "Three years in a row, the men and the women, to my surprise, would stop talking to each other about halfway through the seminar series." The breakdown happened when the conversation turned from describing the problem to discussing a solution. As she busily took notes, she noticed that the men in the room would begin to lament that while scholarship from women was fascinating, it was a shame that there just wasn't room in the existing curriculum to include more women's voices. She remembers one male colleague making the point clearly and unselfconsciously, that they couldn't add more scholarship by women to the introductory courses because those laid the foundation blocks for knowledge and so there wasn't room for "soft stuff."

Peggy felt caught, not sure how to think about this male colleague, who was open enough to take this feminist seminar, but who now was sincerely lamenting that there was too much essential learning generated by men to include more women. "I thought he was a nice man, but this is what he thinks, so is he a nice man or is he oppressive?" she remembered wondering. "In those days, I felt I had to *choose*. Now I think niceness has nothing to do with it."

These patterns are not driven by personal intentions, character, or personality. They are part of systems, she came to see. Like identity, privilege is multilayered. You may be disadvantaged in some ways, advantaged in others. As Peggy noticed the ease with which her male colleagues dismissed the work of women scholars, she thought back to her own response a few years earlier to a series of essays written by Black women that articulated how it felt to work with white women who were oppressive. "The first thing I thought was, *I don't see how they can say it's about us. I think we're nice!* Then the thought I had was, *I* especially *think we're nice if we work with them*." She paused. "You can hear the outright racism in that second response, but that's where I was in 1980."

She began to see how she excluded marginalized voices in exactly the same way her male colleagues had. And then she thought with horror, "How racist I was, and I hope it didn't show!" she admitted to me. "And then I realized of course they saw my racism, but they bore with me because it looked to them as though I was *trying*."

Peggy noticed these reactions that shamed her, but she still wasn't sure how much privilege she had. So she started jotting down short observations about how she felt comfort and ease in her everyday interactions, when others who are different from her might not. Her subconscious mind gave her examples, such as the first one, in the middle of the night: *I can, if I wish, arrange to be in the company of people of my race most of the time*. "I was very disappointed in this example. I thought it was trivial." But she wrote it down and kept going. "They followed from there," she told me. Mostly, they came in the middle of the night. "After three months, a voice in me said, *Peggy, you had better publish this. It's probably the most important thing you'll do in your life*."

It was an honest accounting of the everyday lived experience of one white person. "My original examples had a down-to-earth dailiness about them that caught the attention of whites, because it's not a list of abstractions. It's a list of experiences," she noted. "And the personal nature of that list is what made me believable."

Peggy's list makes me think about the consequences of my circumstances—as a white woman, a parent, a person in my workplace with power—without letting me hide behind assurances to myself that I'm a good and nice person. It gets around all the distracting business of my good intentions and helps me look at my situation with regard to power. The sociologist Margaret Hagerman, in her study of affluent self-identified progressive white parents, has written about what she calls "bundled choices," the set of life decisions about where to live, which schools to go to, whom to socialize with, that white parents make. They make these decisions to set up their children for success at the expense of others, without ever uttering a biased phrase that would get them called out on Twitter.

So, noticing the ways privilege shapes your life is just the start. Next comes admitting, and reconsidering, the ways that privilege has shaped what you consider yourself entitled to and how you view others. Decades into this work, Peggy readily admits all the ways that being white still distorts her experiences of working with people who aren't. "I will, unless I check myself, second-guess and doubt and judge everything, every sentence, every word said by my colleagues of color," she declared in a 2012 TEDx Talk. "I will do it because my hard drive is wired with the white privilege conviction that I am a knower, and that among my colleagues of color, the level of knowledge and intelligence isn't as high as it is for me."

Watching this, I was stunned to hear a white woman— especially "a little old lady with white hair," as Peggy describes herself—say this out loud. I asked Peggy if, in being so honest about the ways she notices her racial biases manifest, she has the impulse to apologize. "It's very white, to think that you personally created this system. That's white power assuming itself. You didn't make it, and apologizing for it doesn't help the situation."

Instead, Peggy's advice for difficult conversations about identity and privilege is to testify and bear witness to the systems we all inhabit, to notice and take responsibility for the way your hard drive was wired, and to try to disrupt the effects of that wiring. "When I run my alternative software, I both admire and learn from my colleagues of color."

When someone else talks about how their identity affects where they feel belonging and where they don't, listen. When it's your turn to talk, give an honest accounting of which advantages and disadvantages you carry.

Finally, she offered me this guidance: "I recommend personal experience rather than lecture." Conversations about identity are about orienting where you stand in relationship to privilege and marginalization. Acknowledging that is powerful, enlightening, and personal. By leading with personal experience, you are naming how you participate in systems of belonging. "When you do testimony, you cannot be argued with," Peggy told me. "Stay with your own experience, claim nothing more."

That's how she and her colleagues designed the conversations about identity that take place at the National SEED Project workshops they run: more as monologues of personal testimony, usually timed, so the focus is on sharing individual experience within systems and listening to the individual experience of others within systems, much like the mode of family therapy that Murray Bowen developed to encourage family members to listen to each other rather than just replicating long-standing family patterns with a therapist listening in.

At their best, these kinds of testimonies about identity and systems of privilege and disadvantage create a record of how power works to benefit some and not others, and of all that needs to change to move toward the ideal of belonging.

"Tell me about your family."

The trouble with talking about identity, though, is that words only capture so much. Words clump us together in categories that are broad and blunt, with hazy borders that flatten individual variation.

In personal conversations about identity, personal testimony is essential, as Peggy laid out, and it's also important to unpack where you fit in these broad categories. Just because categories are imprecise doesn't mean they should be dismissed, because they contain essential information. "Race, to the degree that it represents anything coherent in the United States, is shorthand for a specific set of life probabilities," Jelani Cobb wrote in the *New Yorker* after the death of George Floyd. "Although race may be a biological fiction, its reality is seen in what is likely to happen in our lives."

Natalie Masuoka, a professor of political science at UCLA, told me she often crashes up against these two layers of talking about identity—as a form of personal expression and as a broad category you get slotted into. "The way [my] students define identity is the ways they want to be recognized." Often, that includes self-identifying as a mix of races, understanding that identity is multilayered, often with many dimensions of privilege and disadvantage operating simultaneously. "Students really have a sophisticated understanding of identity," she said, and their vocabulary around identity tends to be precise, specific, and personal. Natalie warns her students, though, that their individualized precision can cause them to miss what can be seen by looking at broad categories. "We still have to talk about the history," Natalie told me that she tells her students. "I always want to interject that there are historical and institutional forces that delineate the types of identities people can and cannot embrace."

In her academic work, Natalie has argued that sweeping categories like race, class, or national origin are able to capture the way a sprawling group of people is shaped by policy and institutions. She coauthored a book called *The Politics of Belonging*, which explored attitudes about immigration among people of different racial backgrounds, and its introductory text is unapologetically direct about how race operates in the United States. "The contemporary American racial hierarchy has a diamond shape with whites on the top, blacks on the bottom and Latinos and Asian Americans in between," Natalie and her coauthor wrote in 2013.

Natalie thought this was pretty self-evident, from her research and from her lived experience. She is Japanese American, and she grew up and was educated in California through graduate school. When she moved to the East Coast to join the faculty of Tufts, she began to give talks about the different ways immigrant groups and racial groups reacted to one another politically. She felt something acutely: the attendees of her talks weren't following her arguments. They just didn't get it. She realized that she intuitively understood race and national identity as a mix of immigrant and native-born communities interacting with each other and reacting to one another. This was how she had experienced identity since childhood in California. In New England, that didn't resonate. Race meant one thing: "a very white versus Black binary."

Feeling this disconnect was frustrating, challenging, and personally isolating. Natalie eventually realized that to be understood in this new place, she needed to change the way she communicated. In talks, and conversations about race and identity more broadly, Natalie learned to back up and start with broad histories about demographic patterns in the United States, who came from where and settled when.

She also noticed people identified her differently on the East Coast. In California, people understood what it meant to be Japanese American; in New England, she felt lumped together with other Asian Americans, despite their very different cultural backgrounds and migration patterns. "To think we can have one national conversation about race that every American could understand, I think is in many ways the wrong approach to talking about race because that's just really not what's going on in the world."

She's since moved back to California to teach at UCLA, and she's noticed the switch back to how people identify her. "It's nice because it's more specific and historically situated," she said. "They have a sense that Asian Americans are not a homogenous group."

The transition back made Natalie more attuned to identity conversations that made her feel more reflexively understood, and she appreciated the less hesitant style of acknowledging people's ethnic and racial differences that she found in California. In her first faculty orientation at UCLA, she told me about an icebreaker question that opened these conversations quite gracefully. After introductions, everyone was asked to tell a story about their family history. She noticed how that one open question allowed each person to signal how they thought of themselves, their identity and where they came from, and how that fit into broader historical trends.

The level of detail was striking to Natalie, as people answered one by one around the room. She chose to talk about her grandparents on both sides of her family. Both were Japanese American. When she was growing up, inside her maternal grandparents' front door was a shelf full of mementos and family pictures, including a framed letter from President George H. W. Bush. It was the formal apology that he wrote in 1990 to all living Japanese Americans who had been interned during World War II, which accompanied the congressionally approved check of reparations.

Natalie's maternal grandmother was born in the United States. When her family was evacuated to an incarceration camp in Arizona during the war, the betrayal stung, this questioning of her belonging and loyalty. Forty years after she'd been sent to the camp, when the president renounced the country's actions, she wanted everyone who entered her home to know how important the American government's apology was to them, fueled by "the anger that comes from being [mis]treated by their own government."

On the other side of Natalie's family, with her paternal grandparents, there was more silence around those years. "It was a lack of conversation," Natalie told me. When they were evacuated, they were newcomers to California from Japan. Part of their silence was due to a language barrier, since Natalie and her sister were native English speakers and struggled with Japanese. Generations later, Natalie is still piecing together what happened to those grandparents and how they felt about it.

That family history shaped Natalie's sense of identity, and also the way she thinks about the categories we use to define identity.

Both of her sets of grandparents were Japanese American, but they had profoundly different reactions and ways of communicating about their incarceration. For Natalie, being Asian American, Japanese American, and the grandchild of incarcerated internees did not mean one single thing. "The narrative for me was always a diverse one," Natalie told me. "Tell me about your family history" was an opening for Natalie to talk about all of this—her grandparents' different histories of immigration and sense of belonging in the United States.

When you situate your experience of identity within family history, you are doing two things at once that can often feel at cross-purposes or contradictory. You are being deeply personal and specific, which brings in the nuance of all the varied influences that make up who each of us are. And you are showing the ways you and your family have interacted with the sweeping identity categories that we inherit from history and continue to participate in today. You are honoring your particular story while acknowledging you are part of something much bigger.

Finally, family stories also help to maneuver around the particular phrasing and vocabulary impasses that can bog down identity conversations. The words we use for ourselves, and the people we come from, have changed through different political moments. Family narrative gives us a through line.

"Here's what I'm noticing that you're not noticing."

Family stories also point us to conversations about how our identities derive from qualities and histories that we can't change, and then lead us to the question of how we see ourselves fitting with those stories or not. For example, the choices available to me as a woman are quite different from those during my grandmothers' lives. Conversations about identity, after all, can also be about transformation and choosing a different way than what came before.

When Michelle first started dating Alex, the man who would become her husband, she did not want a relationship that adhered at all to traditional conventions of straight coupledom. Early on, they had a fight that had her eyeing the exits.

She was going to a bike repair workshop one evening that was specifically for women. She liked getting comfortable with the mechanics of bikes without having to deal with macho bike boys watching. When her new boyfriend Alex came by, she told him, "You can't come in." Michelle told me, "It really got up his nose. It really offended him." Alex also remembers being confused and upset, "taking it all personally that I was a threat of some kind."

When they talked about it later at a pub, Alex was still hurt. He told Michelle he didn't understand how excluding men advanced gender equality. Michelle, who grew up with a "deeply feminist" divorced mother, explained the benefits of having a community of women and a refuge from all the dynamics that can come up in male-dominated spaces like a bike shop, from patronizing tones to unwelcome flirtation. "The world you live in is not the world I live in," she told him.

"I don't think he got it that night," she told me. "He didn't finish his burger, which I now know means he's stressed and anxious." Their conversation turned into a fight, their first big one, and it left Michelle seriously questioning whether he was someone she wanted to be with. They didn't come to any agreements that night, but afterward, Alex clicked on the article links and listened to the podcasts Michelle sent him.

Now, about four years after that fight, Alex told me, "Her perspective and worldview really changed me. I grew up in an insular, gender-normal family. Mom was housewife superwoman. Dad worked the night shift. The pillars of what I thought were my values were sort of being torn down a bit." Michelle kept pointing out the ways their experiences were different. She described, for example, how often she was harassed on the street by men. "I started texting him every time it happened to me," because it was something she was still getting used to after moving to the United Kingdom from Canada. "It happens a lot here."

A year after that fight in the pub, Michelle and Alex moved in together, and agreed that they would evenly split the duties of household maintenance. "By that point, he's on board. We'd had the conversation, so clearly it's all solved!" Michelle told me sarcastically. "It didn't occur to me that we'd struggle with anything." They work in the same field, so they understood the demands of each other's work. Still, even though Michelle was a little more senior and was earning more than Alex, their workloads quickly became lopsided at home. "I just noticed that I was doing more. Doing the shopping and keeping track of what was in the fridge," Michelle said. "I suddenly noticed, and he just stopped noticing. I'm the bigger earner and somehow I'm picking up the slack."

The first time she tried to talk about this, the conversation did not go well. "It was a big dust-up," she said. "He said, 'What are you talking about? That's not true.' He literally did not see it. It was totally invisible to him." Looking back, Alex admitted that her frustrations with him didn't feel structural; they felt like personal digs to make him feel inadequate. "I remember feeling shitty," he said. "She's a remarkable woman, and in many ways I think there's definitely the feeling of, am I good enough?" He pushed back because he didn't like how her criticisms made him feel about himself.

But Michelle knew the kind of relationship she wanted to have, and she was committed to talking him through it. As she'd done before, she started trying to make the invisible visible to him. "I just started pointing it out. I've done this!" she said. "He was defensive, but it percolated."

This conflict kept coming up again and again. Household chores have a way of forcing conversations about identity. They don't care if you'd rather not talk about it; they need to get done. And with each conversation, sometimes more of a fight, their routines changed at home. "He started to chip in, keeping track of what needed doing in the house and just doing it," she said. "It wasn't one conversation. Another fight, another recalibration." Unlike that first bike shop argument, though, now they were working from a similar set of assumptions and ideals. They both said they were committed to an egalitarian household. When that got off balance, they would fight, but the conflict was never about whether that balance was something they wanted to have together. They fought about how they each thought that ideal should look.

"It's supercharged for me. I never wanted to be trapped in a marriage," Michelle told me. "It's almost childish, my wanting fairness in loads. It feels like, if it's not perfectly fair, I'm being taken advantage of." Then life got messier when Alex's school-aged daughter from a previous marriage moved in with them full-time.

"It was a massive stress. We weren't set up for it. We just coped. We couldn't afford childcare and things like that," Michelle said. Michelle and Alex were also having regular disagreements with

Alex's daughter's mother about custody, which ratcheted up the pressure Michelle felt to provide a stable and well-run home. "Alex almost never asked me outright to do any of this. I always volunteered because I could see the strain was tearing him apart, and it's impossible to look away when you see a child needs care you can provide."

So, Michelle pushed through the piles of laundry, tracked the school calendar, and kept an even closer eye on needed groceries. At times Alex's job kept him from home more, which Michelle understood, but that meant more of the domestic work fell to her. Intellectually, she could tell herself that this was the work of a partnership—taking up more of the burden at home when the other needs to focus on something else—but she also feared falling into an old model she'd never wanted anything to do with.

She would look around their place and feel like the laundry was mocking her. It made her feel out of control, so she did the laundry, and then she would get angry at Alex. "I can't put down the constant worrying, the constant staying on top of everything. Because if I do, we are going to slip. And I resent it," she remembered thinking. "I absolutely hate it." This was not a political exercise. Michelle was exhausted. She started contemplating leaving the relationship, and all the household chores that came with it.

Michelle and Alex's fights turned more intense, entering the land of these-are-things-I'm-not-supposed-to-say-out-loud in identity conversations. Michelle would explode at Alex for not doing enough, and he would say her anger was irrational and plead for her to be easier on both of them.

Michelle told me these conversations were confusing. She felt like Alex was challenging her feminist values and dismissing her frustrations, but she also appreciated his encouragement to relax a little. She didn't know how much she should blame her husband for her unhappiness. What was her identity, and what was just her current phase of life? And maybe, she considered, all her obsessing about their household division of labor had missed something essential: that she was the one holding them to outdated, impossible standards.

Slowly, Michelle started to hear Alex differently when he pushed back and told her that all her expectations for herself and their home were too much. "He said something to me, telling me that I don't have to be perfect. That I was okay as I was," she recalled to me as tears overcame her. "He was holding up a mirror to my behavior. He was parsing what matters and what doesn't and really was putting it up to the light," she said. Alex would ask her: "Is it the end of the world if this doesn't happen?"

After one conversation, Michelle decided to stop doing anyone else's laundry in the house. Alex cheered her on. "Her laundry strike was such a good idea," he told me. "It was really clearly frustrating her so much. She couldn't walk past the bin." Before, if there was a pile of clothes, she'd immediately stop and do it, on top of whatever else she was doing. Now she doesn't, and Alex doesn't mind at all. "I can walk past this and think, *I'm going to do this on the weekend*," she told me.

Michelle also dropped off the text chains about managing their daughter's schedule with her mom. She leaves that to Alex. "She hasn't had control with my daughter, and Michelle didn't have control over her own home," Alex said. "It was really difficult conditions to try your best all the time."

For Michelle and Alex, talking about the way gender distorts our expectations and assumptions for each other in straight relationships did not make those assumptions go away. Michelle had to point them out to Alex repeatedly. Their commitment to have an egalitarian household didn't always fit the reality of what needed to be done to take care of their family. That was due to external factors, and also internalized gender roles. They expected a lot of themselves, perhaps too much.

They still have plenty of flare-ups, but they told me the pattern is familiar now. When they notice tension building about household chores, they pause and acknowledge it, which allows them to move toward a solution. "It's clear looking back that my emotional reaction is to focus on the things that aren't done," Michelle said. "I can feel myself try to blame it on something that Alex hasn't done right."

When we're talking about identity—yours, mine, and how we affect each other—conversations like these are where things get really interesting and layered and combustible. What starts as an interpersonal conflict can light a fuse about differences in identity, and then can quickly devolve into a back-and-forth about one of you being righteous or defensive. Identity can be the way we explain and describe our values in good faith, and at other times, we can use identity as a shield from taking personal responsibility for how our behavior is negatively affecting someone else. Our relationships exist within systems of power, yes. And we have choices for how we want to treat one another within those systems. No amount of power-mapping is going to show you who is automatically right or wrong.

Hard conversations about identity, where you talk about all this, are what get you through all of these complicated dynamics. Even when you're fighting, if you are able to keep listening to each other, you can help each other see how all these threads are pulling at you.

For Michelle, it took Alex pushing back before she started to scrutinize all the expectations she had for their home and for herself. She saw that a lot of the pressures she was feeling came from the same kinds of gendered expectations she was asking Alex to upend. They were creating a new model for taking care of family, and as they broke away from those old molds, she had to accept a few more loose ends.

"I'm sorry, and I will do my best not to repeat this mistake."

In hard conversations about identity, we are often forced to confront the gap between how we see ourselves and how we are experienced by others. For Michelle and Alex, from early on in their relationship, they both said they wanted to shed gendered expectations and to divide labor equally at home. Their conflicts kept coming up, though, because they had different interpretations about whether they were living up to that ideal.

"Part of peace-making is acknowledging that we can't know everything about ourselves, and sometimes we reveal things to others that we are not ready to accept," Sarah Schulman wrote in her book *Conflict Is Not Abuse*. Direct, personal conversations about identity force us to take in these challenging interpretations, and to consider how we need to change.

I want to end this chapter with someone who went through that process, who used to be someone who could not be questioned without blowing up and shutting down the conversation. Now he is trying to learn to communicate in a whole new way.

Antonio is white and in his fifties, and for most of his adult life, whenever there was conflict or he felt undermined, he would erupt in "explosive anger," he told me. He was never physically violent in intimate relationships, but he could be mean and sharp-tongued. "I was self-pitying, really, really sensitive and defensive, and just generally miserable to be around."

When his marriage was falling apart in his forties, Antonio spent nights on the couch "worrying that I wasn't going to be able to live with my kids anymore." He realized he needed to change. He'd been in therapy before, and sober for about a decade, but looking back, he said "stuff was just unresolved." His father had also struggled with alcohol abuse and killed himself a year after Antonio started college. As he was divorcing, Antonio recommitted to therapy and started going to recovery meetings more regularly. He realized that he wasn't going to be able to manage his anger unless he confronted the behavior patterns he'd grown up around. This was how he'd been taught to be a man. That behavior had become a part of his identity, and now he wanted to become a different sort of man.

Working to change these behaviors felt like undoing muscle memory that had worked for him for a long time. Like when he was in high school in the 1970s and a football player bullied him. The bullying stopped when Antonio got angry enough to turn around and punch his harasser in the middle of the school hallway. Antonio learned from this experience that drawing lines, and with force and intimidation, was effective. Then, in his career, he moved up quickly as a manager, building a reputation as a take-no-prisoners guy who could get real results. He'd yell at others in the office, so much so that complaints would get filed with HR, and a boss (another white guy) once pulled him aside to tell him that he couldn't protect him forever. But Antonio never lost a job because of his outbursts, and for most of his professional life he understood his behavior as part of what made him good in his field. Being forceful—mean, even—got him the results he wanted.

As much as he projected confidence, he actually feared abandonment and rejection. In his relationships with women, those same angry instincts were there, but his vulnerability underlying them was much closer to the surface. "You get that really primal, existential dread that, like an alien, wraps around your face, down your throat," he told me. "I'm, in those moments, fighting for my life. It looks like anger, domination, all those things. But it's just a scared little boy."

Talking about this family history helped Antonio understand why he behaved the way he did and to take responsibility for it. But he also had to figure out what to do differently when conflict arose. He's had to adopt new scripts to talk about hard things. "I have had to acquire tools and practices and do them repeatedly," he said. It was necessary to "break the cycle, so that I would not be repeating with my kids what my father had done to me."

A few techniques have helped him slow down. One, an aphorism from recovery meetings, is to "pause when agitated." Antonio has learned not to trust his first impulse, which is to lash out in self-protection. Pausing disrupts that pattern and makes him slow down and think about why he's feeling upset, so he can try to contain some of the resultant harm. Instead of exploding, he tries to go inward, to find the roots. "It's work for me to identify an emotion in the moment," he explained. "It used to be nearly impossible for me," but he's gotten better at it now. Like, *I feel scared*. Or, *I feel mistrusted*. Or, *That hurt my feelings*. The words are simple, but the process is not. "It's still the hardest in a love relationship," he told me. When he notices his anger quickening, or "spiking," as he's come to call it, he's learned that he's not ready to keep talking until he's identified the correct words. Until then, "it's just like, pause, take breaths, don't respond." He wants to slow everything down and stave off a combative exchange until he's ready for a more productive conversation.

Still, that doesn't always work. Once an argument happens, whether he's right or wrong, he'll take responsibility for not communicating in the way he aspires to. "When I go too far," he said, he relies on another technique he learned in recovery meetings: an amend. "There's a very formal structure for an amend, which is different from an apology," he said. Instead of simply saying, *I'm sorry*, he told me, he offers something like this: "I was out of line. That was not okay. I was not the version of myself I've promised myself I'm going to be. I've learned from it, and I'm going to do my best to not repeat it."

An apology, he said, is asking for forgiveness, but in an amend, "I'm not asking you to do a damn thing," he said. The responsibility is his. How the amend is received is not the point. Afterward, he will say, "Do you have anything to say to me?" as an invitation, but he tries not to insist on a response.

He also uses texting to follow up on conversations that go awry. When a heated moment has passed and his emotions have cooled, it's been a useful way for him to reach out that doesn't immediately require a response from the person receiving it. He told me about a recent weekend visit with his thirteen-year-old son. It had been a stressful one, with a lot of bickering back and forth. "We had sort of a snowballing downhill weekend of him just being more discontent and grasping for approval and me being frustrated by how I had snapped at him. It just got really bad." When he was driving his son back to his mom's, Antonio said this wave of shame washed over his son. "He's yelling at me, crying. He knows he had really been hard to live with that weekend."

Antonio recognized his son's emotional cycle as his own. But, like a lot of car conversations, this one ended because they got to where they were going, not because anything was resolved. About ninety minutes later, Antonio texted his son:

Growing up is amazing and it isn't always easy. You're doing the best you can. And I am on your side. We had lots of good times this weekend. Remember those? I am always here for you.

Honest and kind, it was an amend of sorts. It also was a love note. He flipped their difficulties of the weekend out of the realm of shame and anger into a space of learning, connection, and compassion. "You try to show him how to stay soft even after it's been hard," Antonio said.

Voting rights advocate Stacey Abrams has said that "Identity politics is nothing more complex than saying, 'I see you.'" Yes, it is that simple. And the goal of many hard identity conversations is the same: to be seen as we see ourselves. But to reach that simplicity, we first have to describe, and listen to, the ways we each have been shaped by systems larger than ourselves, systems that dole out favor and harm in predictable patterns.

Conversation alone won't make the world fair, humane, and just. The words that each of us have to offer are meager in comparison to the long history of racism, bigotry, and oppression in this country and around the world. But at the same time, the world won't get better without more of these hard conversations.

Identity-based assumptions and power dynamics are always there in our intimate relationships, playing out as we interact with one another. You have to start by acknowledging them, and when you notice them causing hurt or injury, revisit how you've communicated and take responsibility for mistakes, as Antonio learned. On a more basic level, as Michelle and Alex learned, the first step to addressing unequal power dynamics in our relationships is to name them when they exist. That won't automatically fill all the gaps in understanding, even in our closest relationships, but it lets us focus together on how our experience differs, so we can decide what to do next.

Even so, explaining and learning across differences of identity take energy and can be risky. It is work that is unevenly divided. It often falls to those with the least institutional power to defend themselves, and, as Meshea Poore noted, sometimes you have to pick your conversations carefully just to protect yourself. Other times, however, if your identity is on trial, you don't have the option to back away. This is one of the ways in which inequality compounds.

So, when it comes to hard conversations about identity, especially when you're in the position with more power, you need to start by listening, as Anpo Kuwa Win advocated. This doesn't mean debating, or responding with your own story, but making room to hear more about what you don't know. Peggy McIntosh argued that it is on those with more power and privilege— including white women like her and me—to understand how we've benefited from identity-based oppression, and how we're *all* wrapped up in it, no matter how good our intentions are. As she said, "niceness has nothing to do with it." Yet often our identity conversations aim for mere surface-level niceness and fall far short of deeper understanding.

To get around this, Natalie Masuoka has found that asking about family history can be a way to engage with identity that is personally attuned and mindful of the ways our sweeping identity categories collapse nuance and detail. Doing so is one way of sidestepping assumptions, to allow us to discuss both the reality of inequality and the importance of our individuality. The best conversations about identity allow us to declare who we are, broadly *and* with precision, to describe what makes each of us special and the different weights we carry. They find what's common to our experience as we scrap to establish ourselves in the world, without papering over the inequalities that make it far harder for some and much easier for others.

Conclusion

This book has been an invitation to start conversations that you feel you need to have. The hard things I've explored in this book—death, sex, money, family, and identity—are each tough in their own ways. But through these stories, you've seen how talking about them—and listening in turn—can be surprising, generative, and worth the effort. Each conversation holds a possibility within, of exchange and connection. Each also offers a glimpse of the simple truth that your burdens—whether you're grieving, broke, frustrated, or lonely—are normal. Hearing someone else's story helps you name your own experience: It's no longer just something that happened to you. It's something that happens.

Still, no matter how much effort you put into these conversations, they will often end without resolving the unsettled feelings that prompted them. That's because hard conversations attempt to put words to unspeakable things: Loss and grief from death. The risk of rejection or shame surrounding sex. Anxiety about our worth, or worthlessness, when it comes to money. The natural, but still painful, process of separation from our families as we grow up. The levers of power, privilege, and oppression that drive our societies and identities.

Hard conversations describe and compare versions of these realities, and each of us is stymied by these hard things in unique, and uniquely difficult, ways. But let me remind you that you are not starting a hard conversation to immediately resolve the intractable. Hard conversations offer you solace and pull you out of isolation. They let you voice truths you'd only half known, and listen to stories that you'd otherwise miss. They deepen connection and understanding. But they do not fix hard things. You can give up that sense of pressure, because that's not the goal. Rather, the goal is to try. When you start the conversation, you are taking responsibility to create more clarity than there was before. Healing and resolution may follow, but they only happen well after initial words have been aired and heard.

But if the words are not being heard, you also need to know when to quit. Hard conversations open up possibilities for vulnerability and love in our most complicated relationships, but they can also reveal when such care is not possible. It's important to have words for that too. Because, while empathy and curiosity are vital, they have their limits. People will get away with what you let them get away with. An abuser, for example, will beat their spouse, tearfully apologize and ask for forgiveness, then do it all over again. People lie and lash out and dodge responsibility. At a certain point, the only leverage you have left is to stop responding to manipulation.

Romantic breakups give us a template. In a breakup, an impasse is reached, and, as sad as it may be, one or both of you are ready to walk away. In other relationships in life, with family or friends or professional colleagues, it can be trickier to find that point of surrender. There is less ritual to it. In these kinds of relationships, therapy has given us the catchall term *boundaries*. To set a boundary is to draw a line between your own experience and the reaction of someone else, so that you can try to see what's healthiest for you in isolation from the emotions and demands that other people are throwing at you. You get to look more clearly at what you can and can't change—and then decide what you will accommodate, or when you can finally just say: No. It is often hard to say no, but sometimes that's what we need.

Years ago, I came across the work of Stanford Business School professor Margaret Neale, who has urged people to shed the idea that a negotiation was only a success if you "got to yes." No, that's not the point at all. As she laid out in a 2013 YouTube video, seductively titled "Negotiation: Getting What You Want," you don't have to accept what you don't want. "Most of us view the goal of a negotiation as to get an agreement. This is wrong. The goal of a negotiation is not to get a deal. The goal of a negotiation is to get a *good* deal." You are not failing if you don't find a way to compromise; compromise can require you to give up more than you're willing to.

There are many reasons to *stop* talking about hard things: to take some time to reflect, to just get a moment of peace, or because arguing isn't getting you anywhere. By stepping away from a conversation, you are not necessarily giving up. You are giving yourself room to see things as they are and see what you can accept and what needs to change.

To step away from a conversation that has run its course, you can say, "I hear you, and I disagree." Or, "I don't think talking about this more is going to get us anywhere." Or, "I wish talking more about this would fix things, but I know it won't." When you choose to stop talking about hard things, you are not pretending that they're not there. Turning away from the pain is not ignoring pain; it's deciding to stop poking at the wound.

Sometimes a hard conversation doesn't end with a strong declaration, but instead points you to a quieter realization of what needs to be let go. In my memory, that's what the decision to divorce felt like—a final exhale of acceptance. But as I was writing this book and reflecting on that time, I felt like I needed to double back, to make sure I was living up to all my big talk about facing hard things.

I wrote my ex an email, telling him I was working on this book, and asked him about doing an interview. By this time, our communication had slowed to a trickle of once-a-year birthday texts. I hadn't seen him in more than six years, a period during which I'd fallen in love, started a show, gotten married, and become a parent. He, in the meantime, had made the kinds of movies he'd always dreamed of, complete with far-flung travel and a home base in L.A. We both were living the lives we'd wanted.

By chance, we were both going to be near Charleston, the West Virginia city where we'd met, fallen in love, gotten married, and left together in pursuit of adventure. I told him I wanted to compare our memories about where our conversations at the end of our marriage had broken down. I wanted to know how he remembered our transition from a couple dutifully reporting to counseling to two people who couldn't wait in line next to each other at the bank when we went to un-joint our bank account. (He'd stood outside to smoke.)

When we met up, his body language and self-deprecating humor were still familiar to me from our years together. He wore a leather jacket that he'd bought when we were together in a Manhattan thrift store. We reminisced about key moments of the end of our relationship. We were kind to each other as we talked, compassionate for the way our younger selves were squeezed, disappointed, and uncertain. But no matter how open my questions, how focused my follow-ups, I realized I wasn't learning anything new. I hadn't missed anything essential. As we talked about our fights from years before, I realized it wasn't a lack of listening, effort, or generosity that had caused our conflicts.

I asked him, when it comes up, how he explains the end of our marriage. "I just tell people I went from, you know, being this one person to a different person. And you were doing the same thing, and we just couldn't find that connection that could hold us together."

That was it. Back then, it felt like our hard conversations weren't getting us anywhere because we never landed on a resolution. Now I see that was the point.

We had talked and talked, in conversations that felt unsatisfactory and sad, because what we were talking about was sad and unsatisfactory. We had talked and talked, until we were ready to confront what our conversations were talking around. Finally, we stopped talking. And that made room for all that would come next.

Acknowledgments

To every person who has agreed to an interview with me: thank you. This work is only as rich as your willingness to share, and it has been such a privilege to hear your stories and to be entrusted with telling them to others.

Thank you to Taylor Books in Charleston, West Virginia, for hiring me for my first job, and to my coworkers there who taught me so much about books, art, and life, including Andrew Hansen, Joy Doss, and Catherine Martin. Thank you to Kanawha County Public Schools for my exceptional education, with thanks especially to my English teacher and dear friend Sarah Murphy Lyons. In the classroom, you encouraged me to write, and in conversations, you taught me how to really dig in. You are deeply missed.

Thank you to the *Death, Sex & Money* team: Katie Bishop, Anabel Bacon, Afi Yellow-Duke, Andrew Dunn, and Emily Botein. I learn so much from each of you and I am so proud of what we are making and building together. Thank you, also, for all your work and care for the show that allowed me to make space to get this book done! Thank you to Chris Bannon for asking for new show pitches back in 2013, and for your friendship and all your guidance since. Thank you to everyone at WNYC who has made the place such a supportive and exciting creative home.

Thank you to my many mentors and editors in radio and journalism, for giving me advice and opportunities and for pushing me to always ask the hard questions: Greg Collard, Graham Griffith, John Dankosky, Michael Fields, Lu Olkowski, Collin Campbell, Al Letson, Richard Hake, Glynn Washington, Ken Ward, Jr., and Scott Finn. Thank you to my heroes, Brian Lehrer and Terry Gross. Michael Lipton, thank you for paying me to write my first freelance piece. Mike Youngren, you gave me my first shot in broadcasting and modeled the integrity and glee I wanted to bring to the work. Penny Youngren, it all started with you.

Thank you to Simon & Schuster for making this book with me, especially my editors, Jon Cox and Stephanie Frerich. Jon, you understood this book from the start and reminded me of that vision whenever I got lost along the way. I'm thrilled we got to work on this together through the end. Stephanie, you made my writing better and my thinking deeper, and your willingness to share your personal reactions reminded me how I wanted this book to live in readers' lives. Emily Simonson, thank you for your seamless project management and vital editorial notes. Thank you also to Alison Forner, Sherry Wasserman, Lisa Erwin, Kyle Kabel, Carolyn Levin, Cat Boyd, Christina Calella, and Stephen Bedford for all your work. Kimberly Glyder, you made a cover for this book that perfectly captures its spirit. Thank you.

Thank you to my literary agent, Daniel Greenberg, for your expertise and for all the coffees and publishing tutorials, and to everyone else at Levine Greenberg Rostan Literary Agency, including Tim Wojcik.

Thank you to my friends and colleagues who have traded notes with me about writing, publishing, and the creative process: Chris Parris-Lamb, Bernice Yeung, Andrea Bernstein, Samin Nosrat, Laurel Brightman, Grace Bonney, Conor Knighton, Ann Friedman, Aminatou Sow, Laura Bell, James Proseck, Carvel Wallace, Matt Katz, Eric Eyre, Saeed Jones, Lulu Miller, Nate Vinton, Kelly Corrigan, Matt Inman, Jon Matthews, and W. Kamau Bell.

Thank you to my wonderful friends who have talked over so many of the ideas in this book and all of the feelings they dredge up: Jim Colgan, Matt Lieber, Melissa Bell, Kelly Jensen, Noel King, Sue Simpson, Jane Bell, Catie Talarski, Danielle Mussafi, Sharif Youssef, Margaret Polyak, Dominique Foxworth, Lesley McCallister, Zena Barakat, Molly Webster, Clara Webb, Max Bernstein, Anya Bourg, Casey Miner, Najib Aminy, Hollis Lewis, Sara Flitner, Lealah Pollock, Adam Wade, Maya Nye, Justin and Katrina Brashares, and Al and Ann Simpson. Carol Bell, our early writing-and-talking sessions set the course for so much in this book, and your support and feedback throughout this long process really helped me through. Mary Gallegos, you fit in reading drafts when you had so much demanding your attention, and I will treasure always how talking about these pages together deepened our relationship. Steven Valentino, you are an incredible editor of drafts and a wonderful friend. I look forward to many, many more years of helping produce each other's lives.

Thank you to my parents, June and Bill Sale. When there are hard things, you step up and lean in. I love you so much and am so proud to be your daughter. Thank you to Frank and Catherine Middleton and Jay Middleton, for your love, encouragement, and support. To all my sisters—Elizabeth, Catherine, Ellen, and

ACKNOWLEDGMENTS

Mary—I have been so lucky to move through life alongside you. Thank you for all the talks, and all the fun!

Thank you to Phurbu Dolma, for all your work and care for our family. There is no way I could have pulled this off without you. You have made me a better parent, and our children would not be the confident, adventurous, kind people they are without your example.

June and Eve, I love you so much. I want to protect you from everything hard, and when I can't, I want to be able to listen to you in the ways you need. I hope this book has made me more ready to do that with you.

And to Arthur Middleton, my love and my partner, thank you for your support and all your edit notes. And thank you for never flinching from a hard conversation. I was only able to write this because of how I've grown with you.

Notes

Introduction

8 *"This much freedom leaves you on your own"*: George Packer, *The Unwinding: An Inner History of New America* (New York: Farrar, Straus and Giroux, 2014), p. 4.

8 *there have been declines in both regular church attendance*: "In U.S., Decline of Christianity Continues at Rapid Pace," Pew Research Center, October 17, 2019, https://www.pewforum.org/2019/10/17/in-u-s-decline-of-christianity-continues-at-rapid-pace/.

8 *trust in religious organizations hit an all-time low*: Justin McCarthy, "U.S. Confidence in Organized Religion Remains Low," Gallup, July 8, 2019, https://news.gallup.com/poll/259964/confidence-organized-religion-remains-low.aspx.

8 *That disillusionment tracks with declines in confidence over time*: Megan Brenan, "Amid Pandemic, Confidence in Key U.S. Institutions Surges," Gallup, August 12, 2020, https://news.gallup.com/poll/317135/amid-pandemic-confidence-key-institutions-surges.aspx.

8 *as Yale political scientist Jacob Hacker put it, there's been a "great risk shift"*: Jacob Hacker, *The Great Risk Shift: The New Economic Insecurity and the Decline of the American Dream* (Oxford: Oxford University Press, 2019).

8 *More of us work for ourselves—more than a fifth of working Americans*: Jonathan Rothwell and Jessica Harlan, "Gig Economy and Self-Employment Report, 2019," Gallup, 2020, https://quick

books.intuit.com/content/dam/intuit/quickbooks/Gig-Economy
-Self-Employment-Report-2019.pdf.

8 *The number of students who have to take out loans to pay for higher education*: Andrew F. Haughwout, Donghoon Lee, Joelle Scally, and Wilbert van der Klaauw, "Who Borrows for College—and Who Repays?" New York Federal Reserve Bank, October 9, 2019, https://libertystreeteconomics.newyorkfed.org/2019/10/who-borrows-for-collegeand-who-repays.html.

9 *most company retirement programs no longer incorporate company pensions*: William J. Wiatrowski, "The last private industry pension plans: a visual essay," *Monthly Labor Review*, Bureau of Labor Statistics, December 2012, p. 318; "51 percent of private industry workers had access to only defined contribution retirement plans," Bureau of Labor Statistics, October 2, 2018.

9 *more than half of Americans told the Pew Research Center*: Lee Rainie and Andrew Perrin, "The State of Americans' Trust in Each Other Amid the COVID-19 Pandemic," Pew Research Center, April 6, 2020, https://www.pewresearch.org/fact-tank/2020/04/06/the-state-of-americans-trust-in-each-other-amid-the-covid-19-pandemic/.

9 *"The less interpersonal trust people have"*: Ibid.

12 *"but to our own need to say something"*: Michael Nichols, *The Lost Art of Listening: How Learning to Listen Can Improve Relationships, Second Edition* (New York: The Guilford Press, 2009), p. 3.

12 *"I had refused to let the reality he was insisting on be my reality"*: Claudia Rankine, *Just Us: An American Conversation* (Minneapolis: Greywolf Press, 2020), p. 50.

14 *"the absence of words is the absence of intimacy"*: Andrew Solomon, *Far from the Tree: Parents, Children and the Search for Identity* (New York: Scribner, 2013), p. 5.

Death

22 *"Show up; listen; nod"*: Anne Lamott, Facebook, January 15, 2017, https://www.facebook.com/AnneLamott/posts/when-people-we-cant-live-without-die-everyone-likes-to-quote-john-donne-death-be/10560414811921611/.

23 *"cemetery plots for families to visit holds less significance"*: Sara J. Marsden, "What is the 2018 Cremation Rate in the US? And How Is This Affecting the Death Industry?," U.S. Funerals Online, July 18, 2018, https://www.us-funerals.com/funeral -articles/2018-US-Cremation-Rate.html#.X6rHQduIaqQ.

23 *that 80 percent of their business is "direct cremation"*: Ibid.

23 *more than a quarter of Americans claim no religion*: "In U.S., Decline of Christianity Continues at Rapid Pace," Pew Research Center, October 17, 2019, https://www.pewforum.org/2019/10/17 /in-u-s-decline-of-christianity-continues-at-rapid-pace/.

23 *that has tripled in the last twenty-five years*: Robert P. Jones, Daniel Cox, and Art Raney, "Searching for Spirituality in the U.S.: A New Look at the Spiritual but Not Religious," Public Religion Research Institute, November 6, 2017, https://www.prri.org /research/religiosity-and-spirituality-in-america/.

23 *with decreasing trust in religious institutions*: Frank Newport, "Why Are Americans Losing Confidence in Organized Religion?," Gallup, July 16, 2019, https://news.gallup.com/opinion/polling-matters/260738 /why-americans-losing-confidence-organized-religion.aspx.

23 *Americans' belief in some kind of afterlife has remained remarkably consistent*: "Paradise Polled: Americans and the Afterlife," The Roper Center for Public Opinion, undated, https://ropercenter .cornell.edu/paradise-polled-americans-and-afterlife.

23 *"After my mother's death, I felt the lack of rituals to shape and support my loss"*: Megan O'Rourke, *The Long Goodbye: A Memoir* (New York: Riverhead Books, 2011), p. 17.

25 *"It takes two people to make you, and one people to die"*: William Faulkner, *As I Lay Dying* (New York: Vintage, Reissue Edition, 1990), p. 39.

26 *"Some things cannot be fixed. They can only be carried"*: Megan Devine, Refuge in Grief, www.refugeingrief.com.

27 *"a problem to be solved to an experience to be tended"*: Megan Devine, *It's OK That You're Not OK: Meeting Grief and Loss in a Culture That Doesn't Understand* (Louisville, CO: Sounds True, 2017), p. xviii.

31 *"I wish that I had had the courage to really talk to my husband"*: "Katie Couric on Death and Dishonesty," *Death, Sex & Money*, WNYC

Studios, August 22, 2017, https://www.wnycstudios.org/podcasts /deathsexmoney/episodes/katie-couric-death-sex-money.

31 *"Our reluctance to honestly examine the experience of aging"*: Atul Gawande, *Being Mortal: Medicine and What Matters in the End* (New York: Picador, 2015), pp. 8–9.

32 *chronic illnesses and respiratory distress simply opted to stay home*: Maggie Koerth, "The Uncounted Dead," FiveThirtyEight.com, May 20, 2020, https://fivethirtyeight.com/features/coronavirus-deaths/.

34 *"could feel prepared about the informational and pragmatic components"*: Kathrin Boerner, PhD, and Richard Schulz, PhD, "Caregiving, bereavement and complicated grief," *Bereavement Care*, 28:3, 1013, DOI: 2009.

40 *"We betray an effort to reduce death from a necessity to a chance event"*: Sigmund Freud, *The Standard Edition of the Complete Psychological Works of Sigmund Freud* (London: The Hogarth Press, 1957), p. 290.

40 *In the United States, life expectancy declined for the first time in fifty-five years in 2014*: Steven Woolf and Heidi Schoomaker, "Life expectancy and mortality rates in the United States, 1959–2017," *Journal of the American Medical Association* 322, no. 10 (2019): 1996–2016.

40 *Black Americans died at twice the rate as white Americans. Native Americans and Latinos also had higher death rates compared to whites*: "COVID-19 Hospitalization and Death by Race/Ethnicity," Centers for Disease Control and Prevention, August 18, 2020, https://www.cdc.gov/coronavirus/2019-ncov/covid-data/investigations-discovery/hospitalization-death-by-race-ethnicity.html.

40 *"The greatest predictor of coronavirus deaths appears to be income"*: *American Prospect* magazine summed up in July 2020: Les Leopold, "Covid-19's Class War," *American Prospect*, July 28, 2020.

41 *Alicia went online and posted "#blacklivesmatter"*: Alicia Garza, *The Purpose of Power: How We Come Together When We Fall Apart* (New York: One World, 2020), pp. 110–11.

43 *A federal judge later called the shooting "reckless, wanton and inappropriate"*: Alan Blinder, "Michael Slager, Officer in Walter Scott

Shooting, Gets 20-Year Sentence," *New York Times*, December 7, 2017.

45 *the subject of one of the first episodes of* Death, Sex & Money: "This Senator Saved My Love Life," *Death, Sex & Money*, WNYC Studios, May 6, 2014, https://www.wnycstudios.org/podcasts /deathsexmoney/episodes/this-senator-saved-my-love-life.

46 *had given her,* Intimate Death *by Marie de Hennezel, a French psychologist who worked with end-of-life*: Marie de Hennezel, *Intimate Death: How the Dying Teach Us How to Live* (New York: Knopf, 1997).

46 *"Even when one enters helplessness, one can still love and be loved"*: Ibid., p. xiv.

47 *"You don't know all the answers, but they have the right to ask all these questions"*: Ibid., p. 27.

47 *"just a look to convey what really counts and what thus far has been left"*: Ibid., p. xii.

47 *"Mourning the loss of one's autonomy is one of the most agonizing tortures there is"*: Ibid., p. 16.

47 *"Illness lays claim to many things and privacy is one of its first casualties"*: Harvey Max Chochinov, *Dignity Therapy: Final Words for Final Days* (Oxford: Oxford University Press, 2012), p. 27.

53 *"As such, I am no longer doing any cancer treatments"*: Shelley Simonton, "Journey Takes a Turn . . . ," CaringBridge, March 29, 2017, https://www.caringbridge.org/visit/shelleysimonton/journal.

56 *"I lost my husband. Where is he? I often wonder"*: Elizabeth Alexander, "Lottery Ticket," *New Yorker*, February 2, 2015.

57 *"what would I miss the most, how would I like to be remembered?"*: Cory Taylor, "Questions for Me about Dying," *New Yorker*, July 31, 2017.

58 *"People have a primal fear of death"*: Alex Ronan, "The Art of the Obituary: An Interview with Margalit Fox," *Paris Review*, September 23, 2014.

59 *"There's no official payoff or benefit to worry"*: Shelley Simonton, "2017 is off!," CaringBridge, January 10, 2017, https://www.caring bridge.org/visit/shelleysimonton/journal.

Sex

66 *"It's so good, in fact, that I give it all the time"*: Dan Savage, Facebook, September 21, 2017, https://www.facebook.com/DanSavage/posts /use-your-words-is-some-good-adviceits-so-good-in-fact-that-i -give-it-all-the-tim/10155757334246252/.

66 *More unmarried people cohabitate now in America*: Nikki Graf, "Key findings on marriage and cohabitation in the U.S.," Pew Research Center, November 6, 2019, https://www.pewresearch.org /fact-tank/2019/11/06/key-findings-on-marriage-and-cohabitation -in-the-u-s/.

67 *more children are living with parents who never bothered with a wedding*: Gretchen Livingston, "The Changing Profile of Unmarried Parents," Pew Research Center, April 25, 2018, https:// www.pewsocialtrends.org/2018/04/25/the-changing-profile-of -unmarried-parents/.

67 *Just 43 percent of millennials defined their ideal relationship as "completely monogamous"*: Jamie Ballard, "Millennials Are Less Likely to Want a Monogamous Relationship," YouGov.com, January 31, 2020, https://today.yougov.com/topics/relationships/articles-reports /2020/01/31/millennials-monogamy-poly-poll-survey-data.

67 *"We are asking from one person what once an entire village used to provide"*: Alexandra Schwartz, "Love Is Not a Permanent State of Enthusiasm: An Interview with Esther Perel," *New Yorker*, December 9, 2018.

67 *"we're likely living through the most rapid change in family structure in human history"*: David Brooks, "The Nuclear Family Was a Mistake," *Atlantic*, March 2020.

76 *" 'make me feel better about myself,' " he said*: Theda Hammel, "Brooklyn Drag Queen Talks Casual Sex and Sister Identities," *Cakeboy*, August 14, 2017.

80 *Paul and Megan, for example, made the choice to get married*: These are not their real first names. I have changed their names and withheld identifying details to protect their privacy.

83 *"Fear of loss rekindles desire, makes people have conversations they haven't had in years"*: Jesse Kornbluth, "Mating in Captivity: Esther Perel Reconciles 'Sex' and 'Marriage,'" *Huffington Post*, November 17, 2011.

85 *A woman named Karla told me about when she was sexually assaulted in college*: I am only using the first names of those involved in this story to protect the privacy of those involved.

90 *"No one likes being passed over, but it's going to happen more times in life than we like to imagine"*: Brittany Wong, "We Need to Talk about How We Deal with Sexual Rejection," *HuffPost*, June 25, 2018.

90 *Julie Beck wrote in the* Atlantic *about a study*: Julie Beck, "Romantic Comedies: When Stalking Has a Happy Ending," *Atlantic*, February 5, 2016.

90 *"I got the message—but not before I'd convinced myself that it was her fault"*: Cord Jefferson, "Men aren't entitled to women's time or affection. But it's a hard lesson to learn," *Guardian*, July 18, 2014.

95 *"Jane, you can stay with him and die married, but you'll die not being whole"*: "Jane Fonda After Death and Divorce," *Death, Sex & Money*, WNYC Studios, June 17, 2014, https://www.wnycstudios.org /podcasts/deathsexmoney/episodes/death-and-divorce-gave-jane -fonda-strength.

95 My Secret Garden, *written in 1973 by Nancy Friday, is a collection of mostly anonymous women's sexual fantasies*: Nancy Friday, *My Secret Garden* (New York: Simon and Schuster, 1973).

101 *"Every time, I learned something new about my body, about who I was. I felt like I was making up for lost time"*: Carmen Maria Machado, "A Girl's Guide to Sexual Purity," *Los Angeles Review of Books*, March 5, 2015.

101 *for Black women, despite their slightly lower incidence rates compared to non-Hispanic white women*: American Cancer Society, *Cancer Facts & Figures for African Americans 2019–2021* (Atlanta: American Cancer Society, 2019), pp. 3, 10–11.

106 *"childlike, unashamed dependence and its gratification by caressing words and actions"*: Henry V. Dicks, *Marital Tensions: Clinical*

Studies Toward a Psychological Theory of Interactions (London: Routledge, 2014), p. 36.

Money

113 *"It's two things at the same time. It's both a symbol and a tool"*: "Financial Therapy: Meet Amanda Clayman," *Death, Sex & Money*, WNYC Studios, May 18, 2020, https://www.wnycstudios.org /podcasts/deathsexmoney/episodes/financial-therapy-amanda -death-sex-money.

116 *"Americans are no more likely now than in the past to identify themselves at the high or low ends of the social class hierarchy"*: Frank Newport, "Middle-Class Identification in U.S. at Pre-Recession Levels," Gallup, February 17, 2017, https://news.gallup.com/poll/212660 /middle-class-identification-pre-recession-levels.aspx.

116 *as a 2015 Pew Center study found that the middle class is no longer the majority in America*: "The American Middle Class Is Losing Ground: No longer the majority and falling behind financially," Pew Research Center, December 9, 2015, https://www.pewsocialtrends .org/2015/12/09/the-american-middle-class-is-losing-ground/.

116 *In a 2020 NPR/Robert Wood Johnson Foundation poll, more people thought it was getting harder in the United States*: "Income Inequality Report," NPR, Robert Wood Johnson Foundation, and T. H. Chan School of Public Health, January 2020, p. 18, https://apps.npr.org/documents/document.html?id=6603517 -Income-Inequality-Report-January-2020.

116 *This survey was conducted, NPR noted, just as the Census Bureau was reporting*: Joe Neel, "Is There Hope For The American Dream? What Americans Think About Income Inequality," NPR, January 9, 2020, https://www.npr.org/sections/health -shots/2020/01/09/794884978/is-there-hope-for-the-american -dream-what-americans-think-about-income-inequalit.

116 *In that same NPR poll, people across income levels were most likely to cite "hard work" as an essential driver of financial success*: "Income Inequality Report," p. 16.

116 *Seventy percent of people earning less than $35,000*: Ibid., p. 15.

117 *"Wealth is not something people create solely by themselves; it is accumulated across generations"*: Nikole Hannah-Jones, "What Is Owed," *New York Times Magazine*, June 30, 2020.

120 *Vigilance is one of four money scripts Klontz has identified in his work*: Brad Klontz, Sonya L. Britt, Jennifer Mentzer, and Ted Klontz, "Money Beliefs and Financial Behaviors: Development of the Klontz Money Script Inventory," *The Journal of Financial Therapy* 2, no. 1 (2011), pp. 1–22.

123 *A couple named Hien and Mitchell told me about a money quarrel*: These are not their real names. They asked that I change their names and withhold other identifying details to protect the privacy of themselves and their families.

133 *the number of bank branches is decreasing in America, closing at a rate of three per day over the last ten years, according to the FDIC*: Joseph N. DiStefano, "Analyst: 20,000 bank branches or more could close after COVID-19," *Philadelphia Inquirer*, July 8, 2020.

135 *She had maxed out three credit cards and was working three jobs—two for different nonprofits and a copywriting gig on the side*: Ashley C. Ford, "The Truth About Money," *The Helm*, January 19, 2018.

136 *She arrived there with $800*: Ibid.

136 *"Not any economic transaction is compatible with any intimate relation"*: Viviana A. Zelizer, "Do Markets Poison Intimacy?" *Contexts* 5, no. 2 (Spring 2006), pp. 33–38; Viviana A. Zelizer, "How I Became a Relational Economic Sociologist and What Does That Mean?," *Politics and Society* 40, no. 2 (June 2012), 145–74.

137 *"People work hard to find economic arrangements that both confirm their sense of what the relationship is about and sustain it"*: Zelizer, "Do Markets Poison Intimacy?"

139 *Published in 2016, her novel centers on four siblings angling around each other as they await an expected inheritance*: Cynthia D'Aprix Sweeney, *The Nest* (New York: Ecco, 2016).

145 *"The trouble with denial is that when the truth comes, you aren't ready"*: Nina LaCour, *We Are Okay* (New York: Dutton Books for Young Readers, 2017), p. 154.

145 *She runs the crisis assistance center for students at Sacramento State University*: "Spring Enrollment Sets New Record," *Sacramento*

State News, March 1, 2017; Alexa Reene, "Sacramento Experienced the Fastest Growing Rent in the Nation in 2017," ABC10.com, January 5, 2018, https://www.abc10.com/article/news/local/sacramento /sacramento-experienced-the-fastest-growing-rent-in-the-nation -in-2017/103-505203427.

146 *That was exactly the case for a student named Alejandra*: Alejandra is not her real first name. She asked to change it for her and her family's privacy.

148 *radical acceptance is a form of cognitive behavioral therapy developed in the early 1990s*: "MARSHA LINEHAN—How She Learned Radical Acceptance," YouTube, April 14, 2017, https://www.you tube.com/watch?v=OTG7YEWkJFI; Steven C. Hayes, Victoria M. Follette, and Marsha M. Linehan, *Mindfulness and Acceptance: Expanding the Cognitive-Behavioral Tradition* (New York: The Guilford Press, 2004).

150 *$85,000 in student debt in 2018*: "REPORT: Class of 2018 Four-Year Graduates' Average Student Debt Is $29,200," Institute for College Access and Success, September 10, 2019, https://ticas.org /affordability-2/student-aid/student-debt-student-aid/report-class -of-2018-four-year-graduates-average-student-debt-is-29200/.

151 *For preschool teachers, the national median salary*: "Preschool Teachers," U.S. Bureau of Labor Statistics, September 1, 2020, https://www .bls.gov/ooh/education-training-and-library/preschool-teachers .htm.

153 *As Pew reported in 2017, compared to lower-income people*: Samantha Smith, "Why People Are Rich and Poor: Republicans and Democrats Have Very Different Views," Pew Research Center, May 2, 2017, https://www.pewresearch.org/fact-tank/2017/05/02 /why-people-are-rich-and-poor-republicans-and-democrats-have -very-different-views/.

154 *"You know, in fairy tales it's a little easy because when Cinderella gets ahead"*: "Opportunity Costs: More Is Not More," *Death, Sex & Money*, WNYC Studios, January 24, 2018, https://www.wnyc studios.org/podcasts/deathsexmoney/episodes/opportunity-costs -vik-and-nishant.

155 *"He is an unusually self-aware multimillionaire philanthropist"*: Dylan Matthews, "Chris Hughes Wants Another Chance," *Vox*, January 22, 2020.

156 *"In a winner-take-all world, a small group of people get outsized returns as a result of early actions they take"*: Chris Hughes, *Fair Shot: Rethinking Inequality and How We Earn* (New York: St. Martin's Press, 2018), p. 37.

156 *"But the combination of those small events"*: Ibid., p. 38.

156 *"We are its authors and enablers"*: Ibid., p. 40.

Family

166 *When I interviewed comedian Hasan Minhaj on* Death, Sex & Money: "Hasan Minhaj's Honest Mistakes," *Death, Sex & Money*, WNYC Studios, November 20, 2019, https://www.wnycstudios.org/podcasts/deathsexmoney/episodes/hasan-minhaj-death-sex-money.

167 *"We were really just trying not to be angry, because they didn't understand a lot of my choices"*: "Mahershala Ali & Rafael Casal: Envy Is a Hell of a Drug," *Death, Sex & Money*, WNYC Studios, June 12, 2019, https://www.wnycstudios.org/podcasts/deathsexmoney/episodes/mahershala-ali-rafael-casal-death-sex-money.

169 *Psychologist Murray Bowen developed his theory of "family systems" in the 1950s and 1960s*: Murray Bowen, *Family Therapy in Clinical Practice* (Lanham, Rowman & Littlefield Publishers, 2004), p. xiii; Michael E. Kerr, "One Family's Story: A Primer on Bowen Theory," (Washington: The Bowen Center for the Study of the Family, 2003).

169 *"an individual while in emotional contact"*: Michael E. Kerr and Murray Bowen, *Family Evaluation* (New York: W. W. Norton, 1988), p. 94.

169 *"I had to say, she's not fit right now," Yesi told me*: "The Power of Yesi Ortiz," *Death, Sex & Money*, WNYC Studios, October 20, 2015, https://www.wnycstudios.org/podcasts/deathsexmoney/episodes/power-yesi-ortiz.

170 *with her oldest son, A.*: I'm referring to Yesi's son by his first initial to protect his privacy.

173 *That's what a man who asked to go by Adrian described to me*: "Adrian" asked to use a different name to protect the privacy of his family and his family of origin.

181 *A woman who asked to go by Anne*: "Anne" asked not to use her real name, to protect her privacy and her mother's personal medical history.

183 *"My natural instinct to confront denial of illness head-on led to disaster"*: Xavier Amador, *I Am Not Sick, I Don't Need Help! How to Help Someone with Mental Illness Accept Treatment* (Estonia: Vida Press, 2010), p. xiv.

187 *sociologist Karl Pillemer found that those family members who were able to come back together did not necessarily have less severe ruptures than the people who couldn't*: Karl Pillemer, *Fault Lines: Fractured Families and How to Mend Them* (New York: Avery, 2020).

187 *"People who reconcile describe the experience as letting go of the attempt to have the other person see the past as they saw it"*: Paula Span, "The Causes of Estrangement and How Families Heal," *New York Times*, September 10, 2020.

192 *"If a person's behavior doesn't make sense to you, it is because you are missing a part of their context"*: Devon Price, "Laziness Does Not Exist," *Human Parts*, March 23, 2018; I first discovered this quote in journalist Anne Helen Petersen's Buzzfeed article "How Millennials Became the Burnout Generation," where she examines misunderstandings across generations, which certainly applies to family. Anne Helen Petersen, "How Millennials Became the Burnout Generation," Buzzfeed News, January 5, 2019, https://www.buzzfeednews.com/article/annehelenpetersen /millennials-burnout-generation-debt-work.

197 *divorce rates in the United States were climbing to their peak*: "Number of Divorces Reached Record in 1981," UPI, February 2, 1984, https://www.nytimes.com/1984/02/02/garden/number-of-divorces -reached-record-in-1981.html.

Identity

206 *"If you can act your way out of it, then it is class, not caste"*: Isabel Wilkerson, *Caste: The Origins of Our Discontents* (New York: Random House, 2020), p. 106.

206 *interviewed him on the show*: "College Sweethearts: Transformed," *Death, Sex & Money*, WNYC Studios, December 2, 2014, https://www.wnycstudios.org/podcasts/deathsexmoney/episodes/college-sweethearts-transformed-death-sex-money.

209 *"The truth is that nothing is impersonal when it comes to racism, or the will to subjugate"*: Hilton Als, "My Mother's Dreams for Her Son, and All Black Children," *New Yorker*, June 21, 2020.

209 *"I live knowing that whatever my blackness means to me can be at odds with what it means to certain white observers, at any moment"*: Wesley Morris, "The Year We Obsessed Over Identity," *New York Times Magazine*, October 6, 2015.

209 *This is what W. E. B. Du Bois called "double-consciousness," in 1897*: W. E. Burghardt Du Bois, "Strivings of the Negro People," *Atlantic*, August 1897, https://www.theatlantic.com/magazine/archive/1897/08/strivings-of-the-negro-people/305446/.

209 *"We are here because you were there"*: Virou Srilangarajah, "We Are Here Because You Were With Us: Remembering A. Sivanandan," *Verso*, February 7, 2018.

210 *"Inclusion suggests you're joining something that's already there"*: john a. powell, "john a. powell talks about Structural Racism and Housing," YouTube, January 21, 2020, https://www.youtube.com/watch?v=7RTQxPfi5qg.

212 *I first met Anpo Kuwa Win*: Anpo also uses an Anglicized name but chose to use her Lakota name to protect her and her family's privacy.

213 *the traveling variety show that Buffalo Bill Cody toured around the United States and Europe*: Paul Fees, "Wild West Shows: Buffalo Bill's Wild West," The Buffalo Bill Center of the West, (undated), https://centerofthewest.org/learn/western-essays/wild-west-shows/.

217 *More than 56 percent of Native women have experienced sexual violence in their lifetimes*: André B. Rosay, "Violence Against American Indian and Alaska Native Women and Men," *NIJ Journal* 277 (2016): 38–45, http://nij.gov/journals/277/Pages/violence-againstamerican-indians-alaska-natives.aspx; Ronet Bachman, Heather Zaykowski, Rachel Kallmyer, Margarita Poteyeva, and Christina Lanier, "Violence Against American Indian and Alaska Native Women and the Criminal Justice Response: What Is Known," research report submitted to the Department of Justice, August 2008, https://www.ncjrs.gov/pdffiles1/nij/grants/223691.pdf.

217 *Most indigenous women who are sexually assaulted, more than two-thirds, are victimized by white or non-Native men*: "Hate in America: Native Women Are 10 Times More Likely to Be Murdered," *Indian Country Today*, August 20, 2018.

217 *there are also high rates of child abuse*: Katherine J. Sapra et al., "Family and partner interpersonal violence among American Indians/Alaska Natives," *Injury Epidemiology* 1, no. 1 (2014): 7.

217 *Native men are incarcerated at four times the rate of white men*: Jake Flanagin, "Native Americans Are the Unseen Victims of a Broken Justice System," *Quartz*, April 27, 2015.

217 *much more likely to be killed by police than white men*: Frank Edwards, Hedwig Lee, Michael Esposito, "Risk of being killed by police use of force in the United States by age, race-ethnicity, and sex," *Proceedings of the National Academy of Sciences of the United States of America* 116, no. 34 (2019): 16793–16798, doi:10.1073/pnas.1821204116.

224 *Meshea told him about the implicit bias test from Harvard*: "Implicit Association Test," Project Implicit, https://implicit.harvard.edu/implicit/takeatest.html.

225 white fragility, *as anti-racist educator Robin DiAngelo calls it*: Robin DiAngelo, *White Fragility: Why It's So Hard For White People to Talk about Racism* (Boston: Beacon Press, 2018).

226 *In an academic paper in 1988, she made a list of the ways in which her social ease and professional success were positively influenced by her whiteness*: Peggy McIntosh, *On Privilege, Fraudulence, and Teaching*

as Learning: Selected Essays, 1981–2019 (New York: Routledge, 2020), pp. 19–22.

226 *she credits W. E. B. Du Bois with conceptualizing it in the 1930s when he wrote of "the [additional] psychological wage"*: W. E. B. Du Bois, *Black Reconstruction in America: An Essay Toward a History of the Part Which Black Folk Played in the Attempt to Reconstruct Democracy in America, 1860–1880* (Oxford: Oxford University Press, 2007), p. 941.

230 *The sociologist Margaret Hagerman, in her study of affluent self-identified progressive white parents*: Joe Pinsker, "How Well-Intentioned White Families Can Perpetuate Racism," *Atlantic*, September 4, 2018.

230 *"I will, unless I check myself, second-guess and doubt and judge everything, every sentence, every word said by my colleagues of color"*: TEDxTalks, "'How Studying Privilege Systems Can Strengthen Compassion': Peggy McIntosh at TEDxTimberlaneSchools," YouTube, November 5, 2012, https://www.youtube.com/watch?v=e-BY9UEewHw.

232 *"Race, to the degree that it represents anything coherent in the United States, is shorthand for a specific set of life probabilities"*: Jelani Cobb, "An American Spring of Reckoning," *New Yorker*, June 14, 2020.

233 *She coauthored a book called* The Politics of Belonging, *which explored attitudes about immigration among people of different racial backgrounds*: Jane Junn and Natalie Masuoka, *The Politics of Belonging: Race, Public Opinion and Immigration* (Chicago: University of Chicago Press, 2013).

233 *"The contemporary American racial hierarchy has a diamond shape with whites on the top"*: Ibid., p. 5.

235 *It was the formal apology that he wrote in 1990 to all living Japanese Americans who had been interned during World War II*: "Redress Payments," National Museum of American History, October 1990, https://americanhistory.si.edu/righting-wrong-japanese-americans -and-world-war-ii/redress-payments.

237 *When Michelle first started dating Alex, the man who would become her husband*: I've changed Michelle and Alex's names to protect their family's privacy.

NOTES

243 *"Part of peace-making is acknowledging that we can't know everything about ourselves"*: Sarah Shulman, *Conflict Is Not Abuse: Overstating Harm, Community Responsibility, and the Duty of Repair* (Vancouver: Arsenal Pulp Press, 2016), p. 41.

243 *Antonio is white and in his fifties*: I've changed Antonio's name to protect his and his family's privacy.

247 *Voting rights advocate Stacey Abrams has said that "Identity politics is nothing more complex than saying, 'I see you'"*: Jack Crowe, "Stacey Abrams: 'Identity Politics Are the Politics That Win," *National Review*, April 3, 2019.

Conclusion

255 *"Most of us view the goal of a negotiation as to get an agreement. This is wrong"*: Stanford Graduate School of Business, "Margaret Neale: Negotiation: Getting What You Want," YouTube, March 13, 2013, https://www.youtube.com/watch?v=MXFpOWDAhvM.

Index

INDEX

About the Author

Anna Sale is the creator and host of *Death, Sex & Money*, the podcast from WNYC Studios, where she's been doing interviews about "the things we think about a lot and need to talk about more" since 2014. She grew up in West Virginia and lives in the East Bay in California with her husband and two daughters.